CHINA
COAST FAMILY

CHINA COAST FAMILY

by John C. Caldwell

Chicago · HENRY REGNERY COMPANY · *1953*

TO *Elsie,*

WHO MADE THIS STORY POSSIBLE

FOREWORD

THE CURTAIN HAS fallen on the greatest philanthropic enterprise in American history. At one time there were thousands of American missionaries in China. For generations Americans have responded to appeals for the relief of victims of famine, flood and war. Today there are a tiny handful of missionaries in China, under house arrest or in jail.

The work of the missionaries, the way they lived is a story of adventure in the best American pioneer tradition. This is the story I have tried to tell through the eyes and the activities of my family which spent fifty years in Methodist missionary work on the coast of China. It is not merely a story of teaching and preaching, but one of high adventure and excitement. It is not only a story of Americans but of China and the Chinese. It is a story that needs telling now when China and its people are thought of as enemies, when we read not of friendliness but of brain-washing and torture.

I have two regrets, or perhaps I should say two apologies in writing this story. First an apology is due my brothers and sisters who also grew up on the China Coast, whose memories and experiences are fully as interesting as mine. But we are scattered now. Morris is gone; Muriel is in Borneo; Oliver and Joyce I rarely see. Inevitably the story becomes occasionally a story of my memories and my experiences.

I regret too that I write too much of one American family and one religious denomination. There were hundreds of missionary families other than ours. There were hundreds of missionaries other than Methodists. All did their part, all had their heartaches, thrills and adventures. All had a part in the drama of China, and all have a share in the despair of this day.

JOHN C. CALDWELL

Nashville, Tennessee
August 1, 1953

CONTENTS

ILLUSTRATIONS

CHINA
COAST FAMILY

THE LAND OF HAPPINESS

HIGH on an island hill in the Min River near Foochow, China, there is a cemetery. Sheltered under two groves of ancient olive trees, here is the resting place of scores of white men and women who have lived and died on the China Coast far from their native land. The history of the collision between East and West is written on the tombstones. The earliest grave, dated May 25, 1848, holds the remains of Mrs. Moses White, native of up-state New York, wife of the first Methodist missionary in all Asia. Not only Americans lie here, but English as well; not only missionaries, but seamen, adventurers, traders. A red Italian marble shaft stands at the burial place of pioneer Methodist Bishop

Isaac Wiley, M.D., his wife and child; nearby is an imposing white marble angel, its wings spread above a cluster of simple stone markers, commemorating the Hwasang Massacres of British men, women and children in 1895. Don O. Fosseman, second mate of the *U.S.S. John Adams*, "died at Pagoda Anchorage, July 12, 1860," "Robert Taylor, a tea taster, aged 21, drowned while bathing in the River Min, the 8th of July, 1854." And Jay Dinsmore, an American businessman of a later era, killed by bandits in the mountain forests of the upper Min, lies near an "Unknown Sailor—may he rest in peace."

A century of trade, of civil war and revolution, of dedicated missionary work, of days when proud Yankee clippers made Foochow the center of the world's tea trade, have left their story in this little burial ground. In the writing, the drama of the century is told. While there are the graves of soldiers and sailors of a half dozen nations, while there are the graves of merchant princes and tea tasters, most of the men and women buried here are the missionaries who made Foochow and Fukien Province a center of religious teaching, education, and progress for over a century.

For the past five years that work has been slackening as the shadow of Communism has crept southward across Asia. Where once there was a great and bustling colony of Americans and British, where ships registered in far flung ports of the world vied for anchorage, there is now no longer a single Westerner living. Not many months ago, Bishop Carleton Lacy, son of a pioneer Methodist missionary, passed away friendless and alone, denied an exit permit by the Communists. He was the last American on the Fukien Coast. Only his cook was allowed to see him during the closing months of his life, and only his cook was present at his burial. His grave, still unmarked by marble shaft, is the last and freshest of all those among the olive trees. Thus ended a great and honorable era of American pioneering enterprise, an enterprise that has left its mark on all of Asia.

Foochow lies south of Shanghai, where the China coast bulges lazily eastward toward the island of Formosa. Near the most easterly point on the coast, before the bulge recedes westward to the mouth of the Pearl River, the turbulent Min River comes rushing into the South China Sea. Flowing from the wild Bohia Hills, the Min bisects the Province of Fukien—meaning "Province of Happiness." Thirty-odd miles up-stream from the sea the valley of the Min widens into a plain of rice fields and olive groves, and in this valley lies Foochow, "City of Happiness," the capital city of the Province.

The cemetery lies on an island in the River facing Foochow. It holds the remains of Bishop Carleton Lacy, and of the victims of bandits and civil war and disease as well. Many of the graves on the hillside are those of infants and children. Among the markers is a tiny stone, its legend almost erased by time: "Abigail Ruth Caldwell, aged 16 months." She was my sister.

Foochow and Fukien are famous for many things.

Koxinga, pirate and son of a pirate, made the wild coast-line his domain in the 17th century. From the bays of Fukien his armada sallied forth to attack and defeat the Dutch rulers of Formosa in 1622. Koxinga was able to muster the largest naval force in history, a vast fleet of eight thousand junks, manned by nearly 800,000 men. Along the coast of Fukien even today one can see the remains of signal pyres on the mountain tops, used by Koxinga's bands to warn of the approach of the hated Manchus, whom he fought to a standstill for a quarter of a century.

Koxinga left another heritage, another important tradition besides that of dissent and revolt against tyranny and alien rulers. He and his men established the people of Fukien as the best sailors of the coast, expert as fighters, pirates, and smugglers. Two hundred and fifty years after his death the Navy of the Republic of China was manned almost exclusively by the men of Fukien. And though the Navy switched allegiance at times, it never fell to pieces. Today it fights not against forces on Formosa, but patrols from that island, alert against the newest invaders of the Coast. The China coastline with its myriad outlying islands today is the scene of a new struggle. By night the thin forces of an exiled ruler slip across the eighty miles from Formosa to strike the outposts of the new Peoples' Republic. And if the hopes of millions in Asia are realized, the months ahead may see great landings and great battles along the coast of a scope never dreamed of by Koxinga.

Inland from the indented coast, the mountains rise tier upon tier until the seven thousand foot peaks of the Bohias drop off into the rolling hills and plains of the Yangtse valley. These hills and mountains too are famous for a different type of pirate—the lordly tiger of South China who makes the province of Fukien his headquarters, taking an enormous toll of the life of man and beast each passing year. Manchu, Chinese and Communist alike have fallen victim to this pirate of the hills.

From the Bohia Hills down the Min valley to the foothills above Foochow are the tea orchards that once made Foochow, and its nearby port of Pagoda Anchorage, famous from London to New York. A century ago the great tea races began from Pagoda Anchorage, with as many as a dozen tall-masted clipper ships of British and Yankee registry leaving the mouth of the Min on the same tide bound for the markets of England. A great bonus awaited the ship which would first enter the Thames docks.

It was a 16,000 mile course then, via Java Head and the Cape of Good Hope. Ship captains traditionally bet one another a beaver hat, to be paid after the race at the Ship and Turtle Tavern in London. Small fortunes were wagered on the races, none being more exciting than that of 1886. That year, nine ships left Pagoda Anchorage. Ninety-nine days later the *Taiping* entered the Thames just twelve minutes ahead of the *Ariel*. The *Serica* followed close behind. That was quite a feat of seamanship in the days of sails, a 16,000 mile course run with three ships docked within an hour after three months at sea.

Foochow and Fukien are famous for yet another reason. On the evening of September 4, 1847, a small coastal ship, the *S. S. Macao Lorcha*, arrived at Pagoda Anchorage out of Hong Kong and Amoy. Aboard were traders, a cargo of opium, and three American missionaries. Five months out of Boston, Judson Collins of Michigan and Moses and Isabel White of New York were arriving at their destination.

They were the first Methodist missionaries to leave America, and Foochow had been selected for their endeavors, because it was supposed to be the only Chinese Treaty Port where no Christian work had yet been established. Actually the Methodists were in error on this point. The Reverend Stephen Johnson, a Congregational Church missionary, had arrived from Bangkok a few months earlier. Thus was planted the seed for a vast missionary enterprise that would in time spread over all China, that would a century later number the country's supreme ruler among its converts.

The land of the Min River in 1847 was hardly to prove a land of happiness for Judson Collins and the Whites, in spite of Collins' cheerful diary telling of the journey out, of the thrills of coming at last into Pagoda Anchorage and Foochow, and of finding a house on a low-lying island in the river which rented for as little as nine dollars a month. The newcomers were unaware that the islands and river flats were swept each year by disastrous floods. The very first spring, Isabel White was to die by just such a flood.

Isabel White's death seems to have created a serious problem. How could the missionaries explain this death to the Chinese to whom they had come to preach and teach of an all-powerful God who loved and cared for all mankind? The long Chinese inscription on Mrs. White's tombstone was part of the effort to explain. The English words are simple, merely giving dates and name; but in Chinese the grave stone tries to tell a story:

"SHE ARRIVED *in Fuhchou with her husband on the 27th of the 7th moon, in the 27th year of the Emperor Tao-Kwang. She was a believer in the doctrine of Jesus Christ who forgives sins and saves the soul for eternal happiness; so she was not afraid to travel thousands of miles to come to Fuhchou to spread the gospel. But the climate did not agree with her and in a few months she contracted tuberculosis, and died at the early age of 26 years on May 25, 1848, which is the 23rd day of the 4th moon of the 28th year of the Emperor Tao-Kwang. The night before Mrs. White died, she said, 'Although I am a sinner I believe Christ will save me. I am happy. I am not afraid to die.' From these final words, it is evident that if a person sincerely believes in Jesus, he can be peaceful even in death; for it is certain that his soul will ascend into heaven to enjoy never-ending bliss."*

The China of those days was a land of disease and tragedy, of bandits, and unrest. As one pioneer missionary put it, "The Chinese are bound and crippled in mind as well as in feet." Physically and mentally, China was crooked. There was little true religion. Men's minds were ruled by superstition, by the hordes of imaginary devils that affected even the appearance of the land. The streets of Foochow, indeed of all Chinese cities, were purposely crooked and narrow, so that if pursued by a devil, one could always shake him by dodging around a sharp turn. Although on paper the laws of the Manchus were just and benevolent, in practice there was deceit, bribery, the ever present "squeeze," and unbelievable cruelty.

The Treaty of Tientsin, ending the opium wars, had been signed five years before the first missionaries came, and the results still rankled in the hearts of many Chinese. Sometimes when Collins or White preached, a voice would come from the crowd, "The foreigners bring us their God. They also bring us opium!" For years the tragedy of China's opium trade, forced upon her by the Western World, hung like a cloud over the missionaries. It was an evil from which they had difficulty divorcing even themselves completely. For in those days there were no international banking facilities. In order to cash drafts from America, the missionaries found it necessary to go down the Min to its mouth where the opium ships, fat with money, lay anchored. It was hard to explain these trips to the Chinese, hard to reconcile the preaching against the evils of opium with the return from opium ships, bags full of jingling silver dollars.

Soon, too, Collins found that the Chinese zeal to collect biblical tracts was not based entirely upon a thirst for the new religion, but rather to take advantage of the wondrous quality of paper used by the Americans. The industrious heathen soon found that Bible paper could be made into excellent inner sole material for their shoes. Buddhist, Taoist, and just plain devil worshiper were at least walking about on the Scriptures.

It was a heartbreaking task for young Americans from New England and the Middle West to adapt themselves to the squalor, the treachery, the brutality of the Ching dynasty. But even so each passing year other Americans came to join the little band at Foochow, or to establish new outposts along the coast. It was to be but a short time until the Southern Methodists joined the enterprise, making their start at Shanghai further up the coast. Some of the new recruits became discouraged by conditions and left. Still others were victims of disease and went to lie beside Mrs. White on the hill. In 1854, the Taiping Rebellion went rampant across the land, Foochow was attacked, and the missionaries who had dug a toehold at so great a cost were temporarily forced to flee. But most discouraging of all, it was to be exactly nine years and ten months before Ding Ang became a Christian—the first convert the Methodists were able to make.

As the years passed the missionaries increased in numbers, the little cemeteries had more occupants; schools, churches, dispensaries, and hospitals were built. The rented house of Judson Collins gave way to finer dwellings, built on a hillside far above the danger of floods. The missionaries learned to escape the oppressive, disease-ridden heat of the summer months by establishing a resort on the 2,000 foot ridge of Drum Mountain, nine miles away by foot but almost straight above the city.

The movement began to make its way inland from Foochow, up the Min River and into the Mountains; or to the south, down the coast. There, the missionaries had to learn entirely new languages, for the Province of Fukien is famous for the fact that over fifty distinct dialects are spoken within its bounds. One may cross a river, or a mountain range, and find that the Foochow dialect, difficult in itself to master, is utterly useless here.

As obstacles and hostility were overcome, Christianity spread not only in Fukien, but out into the rice bowl of central China, into the Far North, and even into the mountains of China's Wild West. The little known Kingdom of Korea was entered, the closed doors of Japan opened, by men and women whose spiritual interest had been aroused by Collins' simple beginning in Foochow. There were not only Methodists in this growth; Baptists, Congregationalists, and Presbyterians expanded their stations, moving ever further into the heart of Asia. With the growth and expansion, missionary dynasties, of sons and grandsons following the foot-steps of father and grandfather, were founded. Thus the Lacy family began its work in 1887 and continued with it for three generations until Carleton Lacy, the lonely prisoner of the hordes of Mao, died seventy-five years later. Missionary families waxed and waned. Today the cemeteries bear over a hundred of their names.

The work, the way of life, was well established in Fukien when a young missionary couple, the Ernest Caldwells, arrived at Pagoda Anchorage in 1899. The next year came Ernest's brother Harry, my father, to be followed shortly by Mary Belle Cope, the 1898 beauty queen of Chattanooga, Tennessee. Harry Caldwell and Mary Belle Cope were married in the little stone church on Drum Mountain during the period of the great summer heat. Dr. Walter Lacy, first of the China Coast Lacys, performed the ceremony.

In the fifty years that followed, or until the Communists came, the Province of Happiness was our home. Here we lived, with little change, the life of the many who had come before us. We fought the same superstitions, the same devils. We bore many of the same hardships. Before our days ended in 1949, our family had seen the last of China's emperors; we had seen a great war against an aggressor neighbor nation; had seen the arrival of new despots; bandits, tigers, pirates, revolution and civil war had played a part in our lives; and some of us were to have had a part in fighting a new menace, more cruel and more terrible than anything in China's long history.

This then is the story of my family, of what we saw and how we lived on the China Coast. At times we lived in Foochow, the capital city, where Oliver, my eldest brother, was born. We lived in Nanping, far up the Min River. But for the most part our home was to be Futsing—"Little City of Happiness." My brother Morris and I were born in that lovely town close beside the sea.

During that half-century which saw the Boxer Rebellion, the Chinese Revolution, two great wars, and the coming of the Communists, four generations of our family lived and worked there and called this land of sea and mountains home.

2

ๆๆๆๆๆๆๆๆๆๆๆๆๆๆๆๆ

A PROMISE
TO GOD

ONE day in Korea up near the 38th Parallel I was talking with an American GI. He had heard that I was born in China and, like most Americans, he was curious. He questioned me about how it had happened, what my father did that took him to China. I explained that my parents were missionaries.

"I know," said my soldier friend. "But what was his racket?"

I tried to explain there was no racket, that as a matter of fact my father's average salary during forty-four years of missionary work was probably less than two hundred dollars a month, on which he had sent five children through college. But my explanation could not convince the soldier that any American would live in a dreary, dirty place like China unless there was big money in it, unless some angle could be played for profit.

Father's service in China redeemed two promises to God. Or putting it another way, he had first had a religious experience, an experience that led him to give up a successful business career to devote his life to the service of God in a strange land. His promise also caused him to turn down many lucrative and exciting opportunities of a temporal nature as the years went by.

Our family comes from the mountains of East Tennessee, transplanted from upper New York and Canada by way of Ohio. My paternal great great great grandmother was a full-blooded Mohawk Indian girl. One of my other forebears was the first white child born in western Quebec. My Grandfather Caldwell came into Tennessee first to serve as a Methodist circuit rider in the Cumberland Mountains. In time he became Vice-Chancellor of Grant University in Athens, Tennessee. And in later years he served in Methodist pastorates in Greeneville, Johnson City, and Chattanooga. He led the wandering life Methodist ministers have always led, now as then.

Grandfather was a stern old man, a hell-and-brimstone preacher, and a man with ideas that had a tremendous effect on his children and his children's children. Deeply concerned about the temptations of city life, he prescribed the out-of-doors as antidote. He encouraged Father and his brothers to spend all their leisure hours in the woods. Perhaps the blood of a Mohawk girl which ran in their veins had something to do with the fact that they became skilled fishermen, expert hunters, students of birds and all else that roamed the Tennessee hills. They also became crack baseball players, eventually sought after by Big League scouts. All of these early interests were to become a part of our life on the China Coast, helping to make that life richer, opening more doors into the service of the Lord.

Father and his brothers attended Grant University in Athens, Tennessee. Since the family had little money, the boys worked their way through college by trapping and by gold prospecting in the mountains of the Cherokee National Forest. It was during their college days that they heard John R. Mott speak in what was called the Student Volunteer Movement. After the address, Father signed a pledge to give his life to the service of the church.

But there seemed no hurry as far as Father was concerned, and after graduation he went into the insurance business in Johnson City, Tennessee. He was immediately successful, his success perhaps in part due to the fact that he was the star pitcher of the semi-professional Johnson City Red Birds. His feat of striking out twenty-seven men in one game is still occasionally dug up by sports writers to this day when news is dull. Whatever the reason, Father did so well selling insurance that he soon moved to New York to become associated with a Wall Street firm.

But he had inherited Grandfather's stern conscience. As he prospered financially, the pledge he signed in col-

lege weighed more and more heavily on his mind. Over
and over again he recalled the words of the 127th Psalm:

"Except the Lord build the House, they
labor in vain that build it: except the
Lord keep the city, the watchman
waketh but in vain."

After one particularly long and sleepless night, the
Psalmist won out. Father went to his office in the morning
and resigned. He immediately offered himself for missionary service, returned to Tennessee, and plunged into
the study of theology with the same vigor with which
he had sold insurance. He had no particular part of the
world in mind for his service. China appealed to him no
more than did India or Africa. So when a call came for
new recruits for China he volunteered. Father had met
my mother in Chattanooga, and he sailed for China in
1900 with the understanding that she would join him in
a year.

Thus began the fulfillment of the first promise, and
thus it was that a young Tennesseean, successful in business and much sought after by the Big League baseball
teams, came to the China Coast.

Father was very serious about his promise. He threw
himself into the study of the difficult Foochow dialect,
into all phases of his new life. He gave up hunting, fishing,
baseball, bird study—all the pleasures and hobbies of his
boyhood. Mother came as scheduled; they were married,
and in 1903 Oliver arrived. The Chinese considered it
an auspicious omen for the first born to be a son.

But there was too much concentrated work and too little relaxation. Father soon found himself very ill with a stomach disorder. He became thinner and thinner and even his disposition changed. He turned against China, took the family back to Greeneville, Tennessee, where Grandfather was then preaching, and apparently lost all interest in China. He did not even correspond with friends there; in fact, he did nothing for months. The promise of his college days seemed more and more distasteful. His illness failed to respond to anything the doctor prescribed; he lost weight continuously. It was perhaps an illness that sprang from the spirit rather than the body, for the spirit remembered a promise made, and the body rebelled at fulfillment of the promise.

Meanwhile on the China Coast the work went on. Having heard nothing to the contrary, Bishop James Bashford, presiding in the Foochow area, assumed that Father was recovering and planning to return. One day a routine communication from the Bishop came to Greeneville, telling of plans for Father's future work, giving news of the Coast. It was then that Father made his second promise to God. For he was suddenly ashamed of his defeatism, his willingness to forget his first promise, the weakness which allowed him to bow to adversity.

Mother was in the basement doing the wash when the letter arrived. Father went down and read her the letter. Then together they knelt among the wash and prayed. Father prayed for forgiveness; he prayed that if God would make him well he would go back to China immediately, that he would never again complain or lose heart, that henceforth, regardless of events, his life would be devoted to the spreading of Christianity in China.

I suppose psychiatrists would describe what happened as purely psychological. But as far as Father and Mother were concerned a miracle occured. The illness ended. In a few weeks Father's strength had returned, and in several more the family sailed from San Francisco on the *S. S. Korea* bound for Shanghai. Seven weeks later they reached Pagoda Anchorage.

Bishop Bashford helped the miracle along with some sound advice. The Bishop had noted Father's early devoted work, the hours spent in language study. He suggested in effect that a live missionary was more useful than a dead one, and that if he wished to remain alive and healthy, he should have a few hobbies. He inquired about Father's boyhood, and urged that the old hobbies—hunting, fishing, nature study—be taken up again. Thus it was that a shotgun, collectors' paraphernalia, books on natural history came westward across the Pacific, to become in time part of Father's missionary and preaching equipment and have a profound effect upon the lives of many people.

Father started out shooting birds around the Mission Compound on Nantai Island in Foochow. He ended up a world-famous big game hunter. His gun, used first for an afternoon's sport, came to be used as a passport to mountain villages which had denied entrance to missionaries for fifty years. His nature study, beginning with the collecting of birds' eggs around Foochow, developed into scientific work of great importance. Father's exploits in time led to exciting work with the bandits and pirates of the China Coast, for all men on the coast respected the American who dared brave the tiger in its sword grass lair. And for all of us children there opened a fascinating childhood, filled with adventures and excitement, providing memories we shall never forget.

Soon after their return to China, Da Da joined the family. Da Da's real name was Gnuk Da, meaning "Jade Brother." He belonged to the Ding (Chen, in the national language) clan. Da Da is a corruption of the Chinese words for Little Brother, but as the years passed the nickname stuck, and American and Chinese alike forgot that he had any other. Father ran into Da Da one day while bird-hunting on the Alps, a low range of hills near Foochow. A teen-aged Chinese boy (not much younger than Father at that) approached and begged the "foreign teacher" to be allowed to carry the "game," which consisted of black birds and Chinese robins. In other late afternoon forays, the same Chinese boy was always on hand, much interested in father's gun, and proudly volunteered the information that he was "washer boy" for another missionary family, the Simesters.

Mother had asked Father to find a young Chinese she could train as a cook. With the agreement of the Simesters, Father offered Da Da the job. He stayed with us for all the years Father and Mother were in China. When they left, he cooked for my sister Muriel. When her family were driven from Foochow by the Communists in 1949, Da Da stayed on as Gate Keeper in the Methodist Compound. If he is still living he would be over seventy now, but we fear that his long association with "imperialist Americans" may have placed him on a Communist death list.

Da Da became far more than cook. He did all our buying on the native markets and so conscientiously that if he ever indulged in the Chinese squeeze, we never knew it. We children played with his children. He became Father's comrade on a hundred hunting trips, and himself a famous tiger hunter. He taught us the secrets of the sword grass jungles, of the islands, and of the tidal flats. He was a part of our family for nearly half a century. Although he would never speak a word of English, we discovered as the years went by that he understood a great deal. There was no excessive formality in the family. Da Da addressed father as "Teacher," and mother as the equivalent of "Mrs. Teacher." We children were called by our given names, or more often according to the Chinese custom: First Son, Third Son, Little Sister, Big Sister.

Da Da came from the mountain village of Loung Tao south of Foochow. In time he inherited a good acreage of rice land and was wealthy in his own right. He and most of the villagers became Christians, but except for occasional trips home to look after his rice fields he stayed with us. When we were in America on furlough, Da Da would work for other Americans or return to Loung Tao with the rifle Father gave him, there to hunt for profit. Each tiger he killed was worth a fortune. He became one of the most famous men on the China Coast, known in every mountain village as Da Da-Go—Elder Brother Da Da.

Da Da's whole family was adopted into ours. His wife, Sieng Guong—Bright Moon—worked with us until she died of cancer. Chek-Saw, Seventh Sister, who was Da Da's mother-in-law, was our amah for thirty years, taking care of five small Caldwells during that period. Da Da's two children were the playmates of our childhood. E-mui, his lovely daughter, received an excellent education, but died tragically, a victim of western technology. She was being treated by a dentist in Shanghai when a short circuit in the electric drill killed her. Da Da's sorrow deepened when A-Bo, his son and my childhood playmate, went to the bad. A-Bo was uninterested in the education we wished to give him, began to drink and gamble, and eventually went back to his father's village as a common tenant farmer and chair coolie. He even forswore Christianity and worshiped the devils and gods of his ancestors.

Although Methodist missionaries usually must serve where their Bishops assign them, Futsing became our China Coast home because Mother and Father wanted it so and kept pestering the Bishop until he sent them there. They visited the Little Town of Happiness on their honeymoon trip and fell in love with it. Perhaps it was because the brooding mountains behind the city reminded them of East Tennessee; perhaps because no missionary family had ever been regularly assigned there; perhaps because the Catholics had been active in the area for years and Father felt the coast needed more Protestant emphasis than was provided by the one or two lady missionaries who had worked Futsing from time to time.

Futsing is not particularly old as Chinese cities measure age. The city wall was built in the 16th century, the older of the two pagodas a century earlier. It is a Hsien, or County Seat, of perhaps 25,000 population, located on a muddy tidal stream some six miles from the sea. The mountains that rise around the city are bare except for stunted pines and grass. On each of the higher peaks are ruins of the stone signal towers of Koxinga's time. Inland from the city and following the meanderings of the little Futsing River, there is a flat plain for five miles, a plain always beautiful in the spring with the yellow glow of mustard fields in bloom. Then the real mountains begin, fifteen hundred to two thousand foot ranges at first, the hillsides bare except for small pines, ferns, and azaleas but the valleys thick with sword grass and bamboo jungles.

Ten miles from Futsing is a gap in the mountains where an ancient pagoda stands; and beyond it the mountains tower higher and higher, as far as the eye can see. The further-most mountains are covered with bamboo and hardwood forests, in which countless species of game birds and animals make their homes. Here and there among the distant peaks nestle monasteries and temples, among them the lovely Rocking Stone Monastery where we spent one summer, and the Bamboo Mountain Temple where gamblers from the length of the Coast come to worship before the Goddess of Chance.

Futsing has one small claim to fame, the beautiful pagoda just outside the city's south gate. Once each year a strange ceremony takes place near the base of the pagoda which is built just above the muddy Futsing River. On the first day of the Chinese New Year, at the moment when the tide is high at the bridge which crosses the river near the pagoda, Buddha descends from Heaven, to the top of the pagoda, down its winding stairs to the river where he bathes. At the moment when Buddha comes to bathe, the waters of the river are said to have miraculous powers. Any who touch the water will be cured of illness and disease.

As the moment of high tide approaches on that day, hundreds and thousands jam the bridge and its approaches, the little hill on which the pagoda stands. Those too ill to walk are carried. The press becomes so great that there are many who cannot reach the water at the magic moment. Long branches are used by those who cannot actually touch the water, cannot actually bathe in its filth. For even if one touches the water only with a stick, some of the magic may enter the body. As the tide is full there is a mad crush, a great pushing, a wild scramble to partake somehow of the day's magic. Then as the tide ebbs, a hush falls on the crowd. The ill and the halt drift away, some to mountain villages two and three "po" away.

There were always those who profited when Buddha came to bathe. The vendors waxed rich on the cakes they sold, on the bowls of noodles bought for lunches. And always there were the healthy and strong who profited by selling their services to carry those who could not walk. The seriously ill returned to their villages, to die, or to linger on until Buddha chose to bathe again.

To the East of Futsing, the country is ugly indeed. There is a harbor of sorts at Haikow, six miles away. Just south of Haikow, Lungtien Peninsula, surrounded on three sides by vast tidal flats, extends eastward nearly forty miles towards Formosa. Off shore are countless islands of every size and description. The peninsula, the islands, the whole coast line is a jumble of grotesquely shaped rocks giving the impression of having been tossed there by a giant's hand. Here and there are flat spots suitable for rice paddies, but for the most part there are only tiny fields of wheat and sweet potatoes set amongst the boulders. Every village has its fleet of fishing boats— and its smugglers. For whether in peace or war, there is always something to be smuggled and a place to smuggle it to and from. In my boyhood, the smugglers brought opium and guns for the bandits; during World War II, they became rich bringing in luxury goods from Shanghai; today the agents of Chiang Kai Shek and of Mao Tse Tung vie for their favor and the use of their sea-going junks. And always among the islands off the coast there have been pirates, men of easy allegiance, willing to fight

for China or for her enemies, attacking friend or foe
alike without compunction.

The Lungtien Peninsula was one of Father's four
church districts. Off the coast is one very large island,
Haitang by name, which with its satellite islands made
up the second district. The city of Futsing and its surrounding hills was the third, and the wild mountains beyond and south of the pagoda in the gap in the hills was
the fourth. These four districts covered an area two-
thousand square miles with a population of perhaps one
million. This was Father's parish.

The first year they lived in Futsing, Mother and Father lived in a single room. Later it was possible to buy a
one-story house from the Church of England which was
retiring from the Futsing area. This was the house where
I was born. Later still, Father received a gift from John
A. Patton, Chattanooga businessman, for the building of
a two-story brick home, set in a compound large enough
for fruit orchard, flowers, and vegetable garden.

The road which led past Futsing, northward to Foochow and southward to Amoy, was the ancient caravan
route of the China Coast. Legend has it that Marco Polo
came this way and visited Futsing in the 14th century.
Much traveled it had been, and has always been, by the
thousands of coolies who carried salt from the coast
inland to Foochow.

In my boyhood all the travel was by foot or in a sedan
chair. Except within the city of Futsing, there were no

roads broad or smooth enough even for rickshaws. Father
covered all his territory on foot or by boat for thirty
years. Then as Chiang Kai Shek consolidated his power
and began to build a new China in the late '20s and early
'30s, roads were constructed. We were able to have a
little, very weak electric light plant. And Father finally
received a gift of a car which enabled him for a few years
to cover parts of his parish more freely. But for the most
part our life at Futsing was primitive. Foochow was a
full day's journey away, sixteen miles by foot and another forty by water. We did have telegraph service,
and the Chinese mail, though slow, was fairly reliable;
telephones, running water, modern plumbing, refrigerators were out of our world.

The life we lived was part Western, part oriental. Our
food was prepared by Da Da American style, but based
upon the foodstuffs we could secure on the market. Pork
we had plenty; but for beef, we had to send our messenger to Foochow, for the down country cattle were
used for plowing and were too valuable to slaughter. Our
butter was white and of the appearance of cottage cheese,
made from the milk of the water buffalo. Vegetables we
bought on the market or grew in our garden. Once or
twice each week we had Chinese food (which Da Da
never learned to cook very well) and we were all proficient with chop sticks. We learned to partake of and even
to like such exotic dishes as sharks' fins, boiled young octopus, snails, pickled jelly fish. Once Da Da persuaded
me to eat a number of roasted hornet grubs, and often on

trips to Haitang Island or to the Peninsula with Father, I tasted of a famous coastal delicacy—cooked sand worms.

While we lived off the land we depended upon far away America for many things. There was no more exciting time in our compound than when the Sears package arrived. It might be three months in coming, preceded by days of poring over the catalogue. The mail order house in Chicago provided clothes, practically our whole Christmas and even the decorations for our tree. Da Da and the other servants could not read the catalogue but they understood the pictures. Always prior to ordering time one of the servants would come to Mother, finger pointed at a picture in the catalogue.

"Mrs. Teacher, would that cost too much? Could you possibly order that for me next time?"

Each order would include some little exciting object for Da Da, Bright Moon or Chek-Saw. Sears followed us all over the world, even to Alaska where we once spent two years. Today the Sears catalogue serves Muriel's family in far-away Borneo.

Of course we learned to speak Chinese, long before we spoke our mother tongue. To Da Da's disgust we even spoke as the coastal people speak, with a heavy brogue easily spotted and sometimes ridiculed by the sophisticated people of the big town.

Our little city was surrounded by a high wall with five gates, with towers and battlements for fighting off of bandits, pirates, and alien invaders. All through our childhood the gates were closed at dark and not opened until dawn. Our compound almost abutted against the city wall. We drove stakes between the ancient stones and made private crossing places for our pre-dawn hunting trips.

The walls were high and the gates were closed at dusk for another reason. Futsing lies in the heart of the south China tiger country. Every home outside the city was locked at night, the cattle, pigs, and precious water buffalo brought into the inner court for safety. Even so there were years when the annual toll from tigers ran to over five hundred people in Father's four districts.

We were not the only Westerners in Futsing. Across the city was the Methodist Girls' School with one, sometimes two, American women in charge. There would be years when another American family was assigned to the city. There was a Catholic Father living nearby, whom we never saw; for these were the days of mutual prejudice. Our immediate community consisted of Da Da, his children and in-laws, and the other servants and helpers who are always a part of a typical western family on the coast. There was Bau-muoi—Precious Jewel Sister, given a girl's name by his parents to foil the gods of illness, who of course had no interest in striking down a mere girl child. Bau-muoi was our outside man, or gardener. He helped take care of the fruit trees, the milk goats, and Father's many bee hives. Then there was Ging-jui— Golden Water—the mission messenger who went once a month to Foochow for food and medicines we could not secure locally. The servants all lived in the servants' portion of the house. Their combined salaries amounted to about ten dollars a month.

In our household there was always a Chinese teacher or secretary. The wise missionary never ceases to study the language of his parish, and Father was wise in this respect. He had various teachers during the years, but the one I remember best was Ding Sing Kie, who during World War II was to become my teacher and secretary as I wandered about the China Coast as an official of the United States Government.

The Little City of Happiness is not shown on many maps. Its name does not appear in the Chinese history books. But it will be known in future years among the people of the coast as the city in which an American family lived, preached, and taught, and built, and hunted tigers.

For us, Futsing was a place of quietness and peace. I have many happy memories of the city, but perhaps my most cherished is of one day during the War when I had just come back, an adult, after twelve years in America. Because I had come back to the China Coast in the employ of the United States Government, to fight our common enemy, I was in the eyes of the servants, indeed of all the townspeople, a very important man. For I had come to help free the Coast from the menace of Japanese attack. I slept that first night in my old room, looking out across the yellow mustard fields to the pagoda in the gap in the hills. As we had done during my childhood, we all gathered in the living room before breakfast: Father and

Mother, Da Da, A-bo's little boy who now lived with us, a new Seventh Sister (for old Chek-Saw was dead), Seventh Sister's little son, the Golden Dragon, Che Chek (a new table boy), and Precious Jewel.

It was as it had been a thousand times before. Father read from the scriptures. Then we sang one of his favorite hymns, "The Old Rugged Cross." It was good to have part again in that simple fellowship, to hear again discordant voices blending in a hymn of praise. Father's strong voice led us, joined by Mother's contralto, then Da Da, rasping a little, and then the piping, reedy voice of the Golden Dragon.

As the voices blended, in Chinese and English, long forgotten Chinese words came tumbling back to me.

"Kie Cai Siang Ngir sang
   Se Dai-bieu. Cio gi Ku Nang."

Da Da ended our worship by leading us in prayer, and as he prayed for peace, I heard a sound I had never heard in childhood days—the wild ringing of the air raid bell from across the city.

Then we ate fruit from our garden, and rice with the unrefined brown sugar of wartime, liberally dosed with sand and twigs. Instead of coffee, kept out by the Japanese blockade, we drank Billing's Brew, made of burnt wheat, barley, and molasses, and named for the Foochow missionary who invented the vile concoction.

Though we did not know it that morning, the end of the old China Coast days was already in sight. The peace Da Da prayed for was far off indeed. But we are getting ahead of the story, which is of the days and events before the end came. And first to be chronicled is the manner in which tigers entered our lives and by their coming, set us apart from the other American families of the China Coast.

3

OUR FRIENDS
THE TIGERS

Tiger, Tiger burning bright
In the forests of the night,
What immortal hand or eye
Could frame thy fearful symmetry?

THOSE lines of Blake had greater significance for our family than for any lover of poetry. Tigers came early into our lives and stayed there. The wisdom of my Grandfather, and, added to that, Bishop Bashford's realization that hunting could rightly be a part of a missionary's life, brought fame to Father as a mighty hunter, a man who dared to face the China tiger in his lair. All the little Caldwells basked in reflected glory.

Most normal adults have anxiety dreams, dreams of falling from planes, of not being ready for an emergency. For me, I dreamed for years and well into adult life of being faced by a charging tiger and finding my gun would not fire. I can remember hearing the deep-throated roar of a tiger at night, and climbing into bed with Mother in terror.

I can remember stories told by Chek-saw, of little Chinese boys and girls who were bad and were killed by the dread "la-hu." I can remember vividly the excited visits of people from the hills, reporting a tiger raid and urging Father to put aside everything to go after the beast. Above all I can remember the victorious occasions when Father and Da Da returned from a successful hunt, the tiger draped over a stout bamboo pole, borne by eight husky coolies. Following the animal was a vociferous throng of Chinese, eager to see, more eager to snatch a a tuft of hair or sop up a bit of blood. Such items had great value as charms against the evil spirits.

Was not Mr. Caldwell of Futsing the famous killer of tigers? In China our name became known up and down the coast. When we came to America on furlough, fame followed us and Father was much interviewed and photographed. One of my proudest childhood memories is of a furlough stay in Seattle. An African big game movie was scheduled in Seattle's largest theater. The manager borrowed the Caldwell tiger trophies to decorate the marquee. We all had free passes to the show.

It was a childhood ambition of all three boys to shoot

a tiger, just as in America a boy might dream of making the big leagues. Morris was the only one of us to make a killing. Da Da, too, became a tiger hunter in his own right. Hunting changed his way of life. It even altered his physical appearance.

For years, Da Da had worn the customary queue required by Chinese convention. One day, when he was rising from a blind to fire at a charging tiger, his queue became entangled in a thornbush. He dangled helplessly while the tiger came on. Father dropped the beast only a length away. That night Da Da appeared in the living room with a pair of shears. It was not necessary for him to say a word. Father cut, and Da Da became the first man in his village to break the rule of his forefathers.

We all heard the animals, saw their tracks, saw them brought home dead. I recollect the day Mother looked out the window of the monastery where we were spending the summer and saw three tigers basking in the sunlight across the road. When Father returned and heard her story he was very skeptical, but he took his gun and sallied forth to humor her.

Father took just six shells. Ten minutes after he left the monastery he came face to face with five tigers. It took five shots to dispatch the first one. The last shell accounted for one more.

Father hid in the grass while the remaining three animals sniffed their dead and came all too close to sniffing him. After an hour or so they wandered off, and Father came home somewhat subdued.

Mother was waiting for Father on the monastery steps. "Harry, did I hear you shoot?" she asked.

"No," replied Father. "Those were just fire crackers at a funeral. Two tigers have just died. If I'd listened to you there would be more. We'll need about ten coolies to carry the bodies."

Americans think of China as a crowded land, with people packed like sardines. The human population is large, but it is concentrated in villages and cities. In Fukien, wilderness is always close at hand. Even among the barren seacoast hills there are valleys and pockets of tall sword grass. As one advances inland the cover thickens until there are vast tracks of virgin hardwood-and-bamboo forests.

While the tiger was lord of these hills, he was by no means the only animal found. The hills abounded in game. There were leopards, wild hogs, wolves, foxes, wild cats of a dozen varieties, deer ranging in size from tiny antlered animals the height of a rabbit to the 600 pound sambar; serow, a goat-like animal with donkey-ears and a flowing mane, and a dozen species of pheasants. We hunted constantly. Instead of turkey for our Christmas and Thanksgiving dinners, we had a choice of smoked or fresh wild boar ham, a tender young muntjac deer, a wild goose, or a silver pheasant.

But it was the tiger that provided us with the greatest excitement, and it was Father's tiger-killing rifle that became his passport into a hundred adventures. Little wonder, either, that the tiger guns became something more than inanimate objects. Father had several Savage rifles but to the Chinese all were "La-hu cherngs"—*the* tiger guns. We children named the guns, taking the names from our favorite childhood stories, *The Leatherstocking Tales* by James Fennimore Cooper. Thus it was that the tiger gun we loved and respected most became "Killdeer."

The tiger is both revered and feared in China. There has grown up around him a mass of folk lore, superstition, and half-truth. According to ancient legend, all true tigers have in their stomachs a blade of grass known as the "pass-over-hunger grass." It is said that the gods provide the grass as magic nourishment when the tiger is too old or sick to make a kill, and that an animal without this blessing cannot be a true tiger.

Father's first two kills were immediately discredited on this score. There were a number of local sages standing about in their long blue robes while the animals were being skinned and dismembered. Not a blade of grass could be found in either beast. The sages announced to the assembled crowds that these were not tigers at all, but some other evil animal masquerading in tigers' guise.

According to the wisdom of the sages, the Chinese character meaning "Lord" or "Emperor" must be found in the markings of the forehead of a tiger if it be a tiger of whom the devils and demons are afraid. Another of Father's early kills, a magnificent male of which he was very proud, disqualified. The two horizontal and one vertical white lines on the forehead were not quite to the liking of the assembled scholars. They announced that the animal could never have been born of tiger parents, but had come out of some strange metamorphosis from an animal or fish living in the sea.

But it was not only the Chinese scholars who sought on occasion to discredit our tigers. There was a talkative know-it-all in the foreign colony of Foochow, His Britannic Majesty's Consul, who made much fun of Father's first reports of tigers in the Fukien Hills. Of all the many tigers which Father killed, the animal which provided most satisfaction was the one we called The Consul's Tiger.

Tigers do not commonly kill human beings, being content to prey upon the wildlife of their native haunts and an occasional goat or cow or dog. But it seems that once a tiger has tasted human flesh, it will not be satisfied with the normal food of the hills. The Consul's tiger was one of these, appearing suddenly one spring in the Kutien hills. All around that area there was an undertow of terror. It could be seen in the faces of the men and the women in the villages or on the mountain trails; it could be sensed in the stories that came into the big city. As it was to happen often in the future when a man-eater was on the loose, the Chinese magistrate of Kutien came in to talk with Father who had not yet killed his first tiger. But his fame as a killer of wild hogs and deer, as possessor of a magic American rifle, had reached the magistrate.

"My records show that more than two hundred and fifty of our people have been killed by this beast," said the magistrate. "Not to speak of scores of cattle and goats."

"But what kind of monster is this killer?" Father asked. "The villagers talk of a saber-toothed tiger who attacks and disappears again with the speed of light. Some swear it is not flesh and blood but a phantom beast begotten of the devils."

The magistrate shook his head sadly.

"Teacher," he said, "when you have lived long in this land you will know that many of us are like children in some ways. I myself simply don't know what to make of it."

A couple of nights later, a Kutien family had just finished the evening meal. The men of the house were sitting around the table, smoking. A child had fallen asleep with its head against the table leg. All was peace and quiet. Then something rushed through the door, upsetting the light and throwing the house into darkness and chaos. The table flew through the air and into the courtyard and when light was restored, the child was gone.

Men tending their herds or walking along the trails disappeared, or were found mangled and half eaten. Crops were going untended; paralysis began to settle on the hills. But it was not until the killer began seriously to interfere with church work that Father decided to take time out for the hunt. For the pastors of the Kutien area reported church attendance falling off because people were afraid to stir from their houses.

A missionary from the hills of Tennessee has little

background in tiger lore, but by now Father was sure that the Kutien animal could only be a tiger, and not likely of the saber-toothed variety either. He sought out the British Consul, a man who had spent years in India, to ask his advice on the best methods of hunting. The Consul's reaction was not exactly helpful.

"Tigers in Fukien?" he said. "Only a missionary could dream up such a notion."

"But there has been a frightful loss of life," Father replied. "And from the reports I get tigers are causing the trouble, and there must be a number of them. I have heard similar reports from Futsing. If you will give me some help and advice I believe I can dispose of the killers."

"Reverend, I don't think you'd know the difference between a tiger and a civet cat if you met them both side by side."

Thus ended the interview with His Majesty's Consul, who offered no advice and began to enjoy himself telling stories of Caldwell's tigers—or wild cats.

Father began preparations for hunting far bigger game than he had ever shot in the mountains of Tennessee. All he knew of tigers was the little he had read of big game hunts in India. In that land tigers are shot from platforms on the backs of elephants, an animal conspicuous by its absence in China. No elephants being available, he decided the next best thing would be a stationary platform high in a tree. For bait, he reasoned that in the manner of all cats, tigers would be much interested in fish. Since Kutien was inland and no fresh fish available, he bought a case of sardines and sallied forth on his first hunt, near a village that had been a center of human and livestock killings.

Unfortunately the tigers of Fukien were unsophisticated beasts, showing no interest in the sardines that Father liberally smeared over the landscape. After repeated tries it became obvious that new tactics, a new strategy must be developed. The method Father and Da Da devised with success, and one they continued to use for years, was simple, undramatic, but nonetheless dangerous.

Father had noted that goats were often the victims of tiger attack. He bought a couple of kids, put them in a basket and set forth for the latest known tiger lair. The goats were placed on a mountain path, and Father and Da Da built a simple blind of sword grass nearby. As soon as the goats felt deserted they began to bleat.

There was no sound of movement other than the bleating and scrambling of the goats when suddenly the head of a tiger appeared in the overhanging grass not more than fifteen yards away.

The tiger was moving towards the goats intent, alert, but heedless of all except the meat at hand. In order to shoot, Father had to rise from behind the blind of sword grass and as he did so the tiger bounded into the jungle. Father's snap shot missed.

The hunt was over for that day. But the identity of the marauder was no longer in question. Come-uppance for the Consul was in sight.

For days Father and Da Da tried but without success. Several tigers came within range but Father missed them all. These misses began to worry him a great deal. He did not relish returning to Foochow and the Consul without something to show. Just as important was the matter of losing face with the Chinese. Already the local sages were talking, telling the people that the American's rifle held no magic as far as the tiger was concerned.

Father was a crack shot. He couldn't understand the repeated misses. He also began to wonder what would happen if he were charged by a tiger and missed again. Then it occurred to him that the gun itself might be the trouble. He returned to the village, targeted his gun, and discovered the trouble at once. The sights were badly out of line.

Father's host admitted then that he had caused the trouble.

"Teacher," he said. "The first day you were here, after you had gone to bed I showed the tiger gun to a friend. I dropped it upon the stones in the courtyard. I did not realize that your magic gun could be harmed in this manner."

It was late afternoon of a long day of hunting when success finally came. Father and Da Da were getting ready to call it quits after having hid for hours in a blind near the bait goats. As they rose to leave, Father noticed a great and excited twittering of birds in a clump of sword grass and brambles behind the blind. He was curious what was worrying the birds, so he picked up a piece of brick from the wall of an ancient grave nearby and tossed it into the brambles.

He could have gotten no more violent reaction had he tossed a hand grenade. The whole slope exploded in one huge charging tiger. The tiger had evidently been working up his strategy for a charge at the goats, but when the brickbat arrived in his hiding place he decided to charge his human foes instead. Father dropped him with one shot, and there at last was the Consul's tiger!

There was great rejoicing in the village that night, and a feast was prepared. After the thanks of the people, after one and all had opportunity to gloat over their enemy, Da Da and Father started over the mountains to get a down-river launch for Foochow. The launch stuck on a sand bar for three hours, and all this time, the tiger, large in the first place, was on the open deck, bloating in the sun. When they finally reached Foochow the proportions of the animal were more those of a well-fed horse than a tiger.

The launch landed at the busy customs jetty. The eager coolies started up the hill to the foreign settlement, carrying the man-eater hung from a bamboo pole. People began swarming from the tea houses, government offices, and private dwellings. Father and Da Da led the way to the Mission Compound. When they reached the top of the hill near the Foochow Club thousands were in the procession. News swept ahead on the lips and feet of street urchins. It was possible to let only a few hundred people at a time into the Compound, so we admitted people in groups in order that all could view the trophy. I saw Da Da near the gate and suspected that he was charging admission to the show.

Suddenly we heard a rattling at the gate and saw the British Consul peering through the uprights. He was admitted and elbowed his way through the crowd. He looked down at the great bloated cat and walked speechless around it.

"Mr. Caldwell," he finally said in awed tones. "I have lived in India and have seen many Bengal tigers but never have I seen one as big or beautiful as this."

"Is this a Tiger?" Father asked innocently.

"Is it a tiger! Why man its the biggest tiger in creation."

"Why that just shows how an ignorant missionary can make a mistake," Father replied. "I have been under the impression that these things were civet cats. Down country we have to chase them out of the back yard every morning. I thought I'd bring one to Foochow just to show you fellows what they look like."

That did it. The consul's sense of humor was not well developed. Even the Chinese sensed that the proud Britisher was being ridiculed. He stared a minute, then slammed out of the compound.

The Consul's tiger was large, it was Father's first, and its killing provided him with sweet revenge. From then on no one doubted his tigers, his prowess, or the magic of his gun.

He killed many more tigers as the years passed, most of

them within a few miles of our home in Futsing. Some of the hunts were routine, if one can ever speak of tiger hunting in such terms. At other times there was great excitement, near tragedy.

Once Father, on a preaching trip, entered a village where a sixteen year old boy had just been killed by a tiger. He had only his shot gun with him. The people were terrified, and he did not want to take the time to return to Futsing for "Killdeer."

Then Father did a reckless and foolish thing. He was armed only with bird shot for pheasant hunting. The village smithy melted down the shot, recasting it into larger slugs. The ammunition Father had with him was sufficient for just three of these home-made tiger loads. The goats were placed out near the scene of attack, and Father had but a few minutes to wait.

This tiger wanted no goat lunch. Almost before Father had settled himself the tiger came into view, bounding up a series of terraces directly at him.

Father waited until the tiger's head appeared over the terrace directly below, then fired twice into the great face just six feet away. The tiger's head was cut to ribbons, but he did not fall. He stood there, dazed, putting forward one foot, then withdrawing it, trying to get up courage for the last charge. Father, all this while, was feverishly hunting through his pockets for that one last load of slugs. He found the shell at last and fired again at point-blank range.

It was several years, and many tigers later, that stories

began to drift into the Futsing market place, even into Foochow, of an entirely new kind of tiger, an enormous man-eater said to be shaped like a tiger but not colored like a tiger. Some claimed it was a beautiful light blue or maltese with black stripes, and stories of its ferocity soon spread through the hill country.

When the stories began to gather substance, Father and Da Da started out after the new beast. It soon came to be known as the Blue Tiger. But the Blue Tiger had a charmed life, defying death. For years he hunted it. As I grew older I joined the hunts, on several occasions seeing the beautiful maltese hairs of the animal along the mountain trails. Da Da and Father both saw it once in the great ravine near Da Da's village, but they were without guns. On another occasion Father was in perfect position for a sure shot. But the animal was stalking some little boys gathering wood on the hillside. Father was afraid the animal, already close to its prey, would injure the boys in its death struggle. So he came out of his hiding place and the animal bounded away.

Father felt sure the Blue Tiger was a freak of melanism, though if there were more than a single animal, as the mountain people maintained, this explanation was not entirely satisfactory. Its true identity was to remain a mystery, and not to have solved that mystery was one of Father's greatest regrets. Meanwhile stories of the Blue Tiger spread abroad and called forth much excitement. One Chinese newspaper breathlessly announced that Mr. Caldwell, the Great Tiger Hunter, had been offered

$10,000 for the hide of the Blue Tiger. Hunters of great renown began to write and telegraph asking if they might come to Fukien, if Father would take them on a hunt. I remember how thrilled we were when we received a telegram from Douglas Fairbanks. I cannot remember what transpired, but the great man did not come.

Others did come, some travelling thousands of miles. An American big game hunter wired from India, offering to bring—and leave—his pack of twenty huge hounds. Father was inclined to accept the offer until he learned that the dogs required ten pounds of raw meat each daily to keep in trim.

One reason for the global interest in our tigers was that the Fukien breed turned out to be a new subspecies. Museums and laboratories were interested in all its parts. The skin, bones, skulls, and internal organs were in demand everywhere. And to all intents and purposes, Father had discovered him.

Of those who did come to hunt in our hills, some had luck, some did not. But whether successful or not, all went away with unforgettable memories. For there is nothing quite like the experience of sitting in a tiger blind in a quiet ravine, or of still-hunting through the sword grass jungle. Every sound becomes magnified, the imagination runs wild. When the coughing roar of a tiger comes from close by, the blood fairly curdles. The tension can become unbearable. One famous hunter bit through his lip as he and Father sat in the blind, measuring the approach of a tiger by the twittering of the little jungle titmouse, the tiger bird of the Fukien jungles, which will follow and scold an approaching tiger or leopard.

In spite of all the tiger lore Father learned and passed on to us, we knew full well that the unexpected could always happen. Sometimes the tiger stalks the hunters instead of the goats; sometimes the trail it should logically use is by-passed, and the animal comes in from an unexpected quarter. Once Father was walking along the trail near our summer home, unarmed and at dusk. Suddenly a tiger charged him down the hillside. By good fortune Father was carrying his enormous black umbrella. He aimed it, and opened and shut it with a great flapping. The tiger retreated in the face of this strange and noisy weapon.

We boys were carefully instructed in what to do if charged by a tiger. First, if at all possible, run down hill. A tiger's front legs are shorter than its back legs, making down hill progress slow and awkward. If deep water is nearby, make for it. Mu-king, one of our childhood hunting friends, had been charged while working in rice fields. He dove into a storage pond and the tiger, disliking water, refused to follow.

Father never killed the Blue Tiger, but as the years passed, forty-eight of the regular variety fell to him. In his later years he began to use a new weapon, the motion picture camera. It was his hope to secure a complete picture story of the animal. He was well on his way to success when war caused sudden evacuation, and most of the footage secured at great danger was left behind. But the animals he did shoot, whether with gun or camera, provided us with fame and added income. Father's exploits attracted the attention of a publisher, and his "Blue Tiger" became, briefly, a best-seller in America. That was the only way in which tiger hunting benefited us materially.

Father's hunting was done in the spirit of the 127th Psalm. His gun did more than effectively reduce the man-eating tigers of South China. It brought us many and varied friendships. It was the key to the hearts of the mountain people, making possible the building of new churches and new schools. It even brought better health along the Coast. For the Lister Institute in Shanghai was to discover the source of the deadly fluke in the human body through a study of the tiger organs Father contributed to research.

Thus it was that the rifle, together with the Bible, became a formidable weapon against the superstitions and diseases of the China Coast.

4

THE SEA CAT

WHEN Father made up his mind to transplant his boyhood interests from the United States to China he did so with a vengeance. He made the woods and waters of Fukien Province his happy hunting ground. I can well imagine that the Caldwell youngsters, swooping about with butterfly nets, stirred up plenty of comment in Tennessee, but how much more talk such goings on must have caused in China! From our earliest childhood we scoured the hills and valleys in search of wildlife. Each of us received a butterfly net and, when the age of discretion came, a tin of potassium cyanide for killing every variety of insect. During the nesting seasons, we climbed the highest trees and struggled through miles of sword grass jungles in search of birds' eggs.

Until the missionaries came along, the natural history of China was completely unknown to the Western World. Little collecting and exploring had been done, and nothing had been written. The Chinese are an unscientific people and have seldom made the slightest attempt to discriminate between fact and fiction. If a man-eating tiger appeared in the hills it was commonly believed that a devil or dragon was on the loose. Myths, strange and exciting, grew up about animals, birds, and fish. It became a challenge to Father to get beyond the myth, to ferret out the truth behind the superstition, and so to increase, even in some slight measure, the knowledge of China's remarkable flora and fauna.

Our scientific investigations roused considerable anxiety among the Chinese, and must have greatly embarrassed our friends and servants. It was rumored that the "foreign devils" ate bugs and butterflies, that the juices of the insects we collected and the yolks of the birds' eggs we stole were used to make powerful white man's medicine. From time to time the leaders of anti-foreign movements would call attention to our activities, attempting to stir up fear and suspicion among the ignorant. But they were not particularly successful. The Chinese people are basically tolerant, and willingly accept the foibles of others.

When our collecting fever began to be noticed in the States, when our specimens were sought after and actually paid for by American museums and dealers, we could offer money to the Chinese to help us in our search for rare birds' eggs, and insects. As long as cash was involved the Chinese cared less and less what we did with the material. They even cooperated whole-heartedly, and the results were most helpful, though often startling.

Centuries ago there was a noted sage of Foochow by the name of Han Yu. He was a very educated man, famous throughout the land for his scholarship and wisdom. Then one day when he saved the city from a deadly scourge he became a popular hero also.

According to the legend, crocodiles began to infest the Min River. Cattle were snatched from the water's edge, unwary fishermen dragged from their boats, children playing on the river banks vanished from sight. Hunters with spears and bows went forth to battle the crocodiles but to no avail. Finally, Han Yu the Wise was consulted, and being literary he solved the problem according to his talents. He wrote beautiful diplomatic notes to the crocodiles protesting the evil of their ways and petitioning them to "Quit the Land of Happiness" and find food elsewhere. The epistles were tied to goats and pigs and the animals thrown into the currents of the Min River at the Bridge of Ten Thousand Ages. Surely the crocodiles must have picked up the appeals to their better selves, for it is told that they left the Min at once, and the people rejoiced. The story of Han Yu's achievement is told in Fukien to this day.

But apparently the effect of his words on the crocodiles themselves wore off in time. When I was a small boy in Futsing the trouble was beginning all over again.

Some Min River monster was taking its toll of human sacrifice. The inevitable stories of demons and devils were growing apace.

Father became intrigued. He had recently bested his critics by killing his first tiger. He decided to tackle the unknown. Crocodiles are not supposed to be found in Fukien waters, so Father figured a shark might have inadvertently worked its way upstream. He also reasoned that any creature that liked meat could be caught with meat.

He had a blacksmith forge an enormous iron hook with a shank fully twelve inches long. He baited the hook with goat and dog meat, and began trolling up and down the Min River. Curious crowds lined the river banks to watch. For days on end we dragged dead goats and dogs up and down the Min with no luck. Nothing bit. But strangely enough the killings ceased entirely. Possibly terrified by all the disturbance on land and water, whatever it was took the hint and departed. But the river folk were tremendously impressed. Teacher Caldwell had worked magic.

As for Father, his curiosity was never wholly satisfied, though much later he tentatively concluded that the monster must have been an Estuarian Crocodile as in the time of Han Yu. Estuarian Crocodiles are native to much of South Asia and have occasionally been known to stray up the coast as far as the Fukien river mouth.

Ornithology was our greatest joy, and we made a real contribution in that field. Imagine the thrill of finding ourselves in a land full of hundreds of species of unrecorded exotic birds. Whenever we went into the hill country, or even right in our own compound, beautiful new birdsongs tantalized our ear, bright strange colors captivated our eye. Many times we failed to see the singer, much less identify him.

It is these days of bird study that bring back my clearest memory of Father as a man. He is nearly six feet tall, not a big man but so intensely alive, bursting with enthusiasm, strenuously active. He is dressed in khaki, pith sun helmet on his head, his face is ruddy, sun-burned and intent. At any moment he might climb a tall tree or clamber up a cliff in search of game or specimen. On our expeditions he was silent except to point out a strange bird or animal along the path. He could walk thirty miles in a day and he could then, and still can, outwalk me. He was sometimes impatient with my slowness and with my fears but the impatience never lasted long. He could be boyish in his enthusiasm for some new discovery yet vigorous in his disappointment at a shot missed or a new bird glimpsed and lost in the jungle. I never saw him out of sorts with Da Da but I have heard him almost shout with eloquent denunciation of those who would trick us, of those who failed to fulfill a bargain.

Above all I remember Father as curious of everything unknown, his active mind never content until all avenues of investigation had been followed. From him I learned not only a great love of the out-of-doors but to be curious myself, to be accurate, never to be content until I was certain that I had the answer in my grasp.

I never heard Father use bad language of any description. But my cousin Eden maintains, and the story persists, that once in his life Father swore.

Eden and Father were collecting and Eden was walking along a rice paddy when Father shouted to him.

"Eden, don't move! There is a blankety viper right in front of you!"

Eden froze and Father killed the viper. Whether or not any bad language was used, I do not know. While I cannot be sure, I think the good Lord would forgive him. Eden's snake was a bamboo viper—the Cha-mui-da, more deadly than any other species known to science. I do know Father was capable of responding quickly to any situation.

I remember the time we had tracking down a night bird whose soft three-noted whistle charmed us. The country folk had told Father that the whistler in the dark was a tiny spirit bird, with feathers of gold. They said it hung upside down and whistled till the blood dropped from its beak, then rested for a few moments and began again. So we called it the "Golden Owl" for the time being, and spent long hours outdoors at night, with a shotgun, trying to catch a glimpse of enough movement to shoot at. Often we would be standing under the very tree where the bird was calling, and yet be unable to hear or see the faintest stir of leaf or wing.

We had about decided to believe it was a spirit indeed when our moment came. One bright moonlight evening, hearing it close to the house, Father went out once again with loaded gun. As he approached the tree from whence the call came, he thought he caught a flutter in the topmost branches. He fired. A tiny mouse-colored thing, not much bigger than a sparrow, fell at his feet. On examination, it actually turned out to be an owl, the Pygmy Owlet, smallest of all the species. We couldn't believe that anything so little could have so loud a voice. Its feathers were not of gold, and it had never hung upside down, or dripped blood, but it was a truly exciting discovery all the same.

But now and then our passion for finding new birds led us into danger. Once, on a tiger hunting expedition into the mountains west of Futsing we gave up tiger for birds just long enough to be almost lost. We had spotted a brilliantly feathered creature, glossy black and red, far off among the trees. It had a song easily imitated and Father was able to whistle it up within shooting range. He replaced the buckshot with birdshot, and on the first shot the bird came tumbling down into a thick patch of sword grass in a pit-like depression at our feet. Thoughtlessly, we dropped our guns and slid down the steep incline.

We found the bird but had no more than picked it up when we heard the unmistakable and blood-chilling grunt of a tiger. It could not have been more than a dozen feet away, so close that we could even hear the gurgle in the throat that follows the grunt. The sound was not pleasant.

Father shouted at me.

"John get back up on the bank quickly."

I did not need his warning. I was already well on my way.

But then I began to call fearfully to him.

"Help me Dad—I can't make it alone—I'm stuck!"

Our unloaded guns were on the brow above. The bank was loose earth. But we started clawing our way up desperately. Bushes and sword grass came away in our hands. We slid back. We tried again. I was absolutely sure the tiger was breathing down my neck.

When we finally cleared the edge, snatched up our weapons and turned, the tiger was nowhere in sight. One look at the opposite side of the ravine proved he had made as mad a scramble for safety as we had. Gratefully, Father and I counted our blessings, not least of which was one of the most beautiful birds of the South China mountains, the Crested Hill Cuckoo. Father had held on to that, tiger or no tiger.

There were many islands off the coast of Fukien Province where myriads of sandpipers, plovers, terns, and seagulls nested, and one spring I was allowed to stay out of high school to help in making a collection of their eggs ordered by a Museum in Cleveland.

Our greatest haul came from Haitang Island, where we had the opportunity to spend two weeks. Haitang was one of Father's four districts, and a center of Methodist work with over twenty active churches. A revival was scheduled in one of its villages. The village lay on the edge of a wide grassy plain known as the "Seven Li Flats," and while Father preached every afternoon and evening, I roamed the plains, the rocky hills, and the beaches and sand dunes in search of birds' eggs.

In an effort to gather all the specimens needed, we had

the local preacher post a notice in the village market place:

"Foreign Teacher Caldwell wishes to collect the eggs of the rare birds found on this island. One copper cash will be paid to those who bring eggs to the Teacher, providing the eggs are in full sets, with information as to where collected."

We hoped in this way to obtain a few sets of some of the rarer birds nesting only on the outlying inlets and beaches.

We were completely unprepared for the avalanche that followed. I am convinced that every one of Haitang's thousands of farmers and fishermen quit regular work and went egg hunting. Momentarily the fresh—and not-so-fresh—eggs arrived. There were eggs too common to preserve, there were eggs we could not identify, there were eggs on the verge of hatching which were as good as no good. For scientific purposes eggs are "blown," and obviously an egg cannot be blown out if the embryo is well developed. We were staying in a private home built around a big courtyard, and as the flow of eggs increased we had to use the yard for storage. It was hot and humid and the eggs about to hatch went right on hatching without a mother's aid. Soon we had plovers, sandpipers, oyster catchers, terns, and seagulls cheeping and running about in all directions.

The hatching and cheeping continued at night, too. Finally, in desperation we sent runners round the island posting a new notice:

"The Foreign Teachers thank the people of
Haitang for their cooperation in bringing many
interesting eggs. But please no more eggs."

One of the wonders of Haitang is the huge "Thirty-
Six-Legged Lake" that sprawls in the center of the island, reaching out in places to within a few hundred
yards from the sea. The waters of the lake are clear and
cold and abound with fish and aquatic animals. Fed by
mighty bottom springs, the lake slowly fills up and backs
into its many arms and legs which stretch far among the
jagged hills. Every seven years, according to the Haitang
folk, the pressure becomes so fierce that the foot of the
most easterly leg is blown off and the lake drains naturally
and tumultously into the sea. This "blowing off," as it is
called, is a great event in the life of the people. Thousands
come armed with tridents, spears, hoes, and clubs to re-
trieve the tons of eel, fish, otter, and mink that are carried
out seaward across the sand.

The Thirty-Six-Legged Lake had blown its foot shortly before our arrival that year, and many strange animals
and fish were reported being caught just off the shore.
Reports came of a particularly strange creature that had
been taken in a fisherman's net. The description of the
animal was so intriguing that Father sent word he would
like to see it. Unfortunately it had already become the
property of a prominent Confucian scholar known in
Haitang for his interest in making money. He had heard
of Father's interest in all things strange, so he played hard

to get and would not allow us to see the animal for four days. By then he considered us ripe for a big price and sent the animal over.

It was indeed an unusual specimen, not an otter, not a seal, not like anything we had ever seen or read about. It had a rat-like head with protruding flattened jaws and ugly teeth. It was the size of a house cat. The only attractive thing about it was its lovely fur. Our best guess was that it was a huge swimming shrew, although we had never heard of the existence of such an animal. It could be an important scientific find. As soon as it was noised abroad that Mr. Caldwell, the great scientist, could not identify it, the price sky-rocketed.

In keeping with Chinese custom, Father began to maneuver and bargain through a middle man, appointing the Methodist District Superintendent to the job. So successful were this man's efforts that after several days of careful negotiations the price came down to that of a pig (three dollars) which Father willingly paid. The animal was brought to the Methodist church and a small boy dispatched to the market to buy fresh, live fish—the only food the little beast would take. The boy carelessly laid his hand on top of the cage and like a flash the beast lunged at an exposed finger. We now had the added expense of paying the boy's medical bills.

But our troubles were just beginning. We put the cage in an upstairs room of the church for the night. The animal was fed and bedded down in complete security— or so we thought. But we had not reckoned with its teeth.

By morning the "shrew" had gnawed through the cage and through the window sill and was gone. Unfortunately, our "mediator" had not paid the purchase price the day before. When he called on the scholar to make payment he innocently remarked that the animal had escaped. That gave our wily sage a bright idea. He refused to accept any money. He shouted that he had been tricked in the first place, that the animal had never been really sold, that it still belonged to him, and now, since the foreign devil had allowed it to escape, great damages must be paid.

Two hours later a heavily sealed envelope arrived at the church, addressed to Father. The enclosed document was a claim for damages, listing the various parts of the animal (named a Sea Cat in the claim) and the value of each part. It was an imposing bill of particulars. Highest in price came the testicles at fifty dollars each, then the liver, the spleen, and finally the skin. In each case, elaborate reasons were given for the price asked: A few drops of medicine made from the liver would make it possible for fishermen and sea captains to see a distance of three miles through dense fog. Seafarers wearing collars made from the skin would be able to hear the pounding of waves on underwater shoals five miles away. Part by part this mysterious pet of the Sea Goddess Ma Cu was listed and priced. The total bill came to a staggering $500.

But surprisingly enough, when it became known that the scholar had presented such a ridiculous claim, the

whole town sided with Father in the ensuing controversy. Prominent merchants, Christian and non-Christian, came to offer help in fighting the case. Representatives of the Chamber of Commerce rendered an official
apology in the name of the island.

One does not hurry a business or legal transaction in
China. Father did nothing. A preaching service was
scheduled for that night at the Tangtau Church, and an
unusually vast crowd arrived at the church, expecting
perhaps to hear Father invoke the wrath of his God
against the scholar. Father was in excellent form as far as
the gospel went, but he never even mentioned the Sea
Cat. At the close of the sermon he asked as usual for those
who wished to become Christians to step forward.

A large number came up the aisle, but just at the moment when the service was most solemn an excited young
man rushed into the Church.

"The Sea Cat," he shouted, "the Sea Cat—I saw it."

The service broke up. The District Superintendent
threw off his long robe and rushed out with the congrega-
tion at his heels scrambling in every direction. Father
hurried to our sleeping quarters in the bell tower room
to get his flashlight.

Down the street we found a seething, tumultuous
throng. The Superintendent was down on all fours jam-
ming a sack over the mouth of a foul drain. Other men
were laboriously removing sections of the drain pipe. A
shout went up when the animal was sighted briefly. Men

pounded Father on the back and shouted congratulations. Ardent members of the church began to sing
"Praise God from Whom All Blessings Flow."

A great roar of triumph went up as the last section of
the pipe was removed and the snarling animal captured
in the sack.

By mid-afternoon of the next day the value of the Sea
Cat had again diminished greatly and Father was pressed
to accept it for the original price. But to my amazement
Father declared that negotiations were off and he could
not accept the animal at any price. "Face," and the good
of his work, were at stake. His stature, his future activities on Haitang Island, would depend upon keeping face.

It seemed awfully strange to me then that such a rare
animal, which might definitely have increased Father's
reputation as a scientist, must be sacrificed to a missionary's prestige. But the decision must have been the right
one. Haitang was to become one of the bulwarks of
Christianity on the China Coast. And any member of our
family, indeed any American, has always been warmly
welcomed there.

More often than not our scientific work met the superstitions of old China head-on. And once, when we wished
to secure a series of eggs of the Chinese House Swallow,
we even found it necessary to practice a bit of the lar-
ceny Father preached against.

The Chinese feel the same way about the arrival and
nesting of swallows that the Dutch feel about storks: a
house which has a swallow's nest under its eaves is a lucky

house. The birds are omens of happiness and good fortune. We asked permission of a dozen merchants on the main street of Gnu-keh village to collect swallow's eggs but were always refused. We explained that the swallows would build another nest immediately, that they would not leave the spot, but all to no avail. So I waited until late at night when the shops were closed and shuttered, then I crept along the street and hijacked the eggs I needed.

The foreign settlements of Foochow lies on a high hill on Nantai Island above the Min River. Far below, along the banks of the river, is a busy commercial street and busier market place. Between the market place and the residences above, a number of giant pines sprout from the hillside, and usually they were a nesting haven of the Black-eared Kite, which is the common scavenging hawk of the China Coast.

Father decided he must have a set of the Kite's eggs. One day he started climbing a big pine in which there was a bulky Kite's nest. By the time he was two-thirds of the way up Mother Kite became alarmed. She made a screaming, clawing dive at Father and ripped into his foreign style hat which came away in her talons. She bore it off in triumph, biting it fiercely as she flew. When she was directly over the market place she discovered that her real enemy was still approaching her nest. She dropped the hat and swept in for another attack.

The hat sailed slowly down, gliding from side to side, and landed squarely on top of a basket of cabbage in the center of the market place. Immediately the shrill tumult of haggling voices was stilled. Everyone looked skyward, but there was nothing to be seen. The silence continued for a few moments while the marketers stood thunder-struck at the strange appearance of a foreign devil's hat out of the sky. Then all hesitation vanished and there was a wild exodus as men, women, and children fled in terror, leaving everything behind in their haste to escape the evil portent.

What had been started as a hobby gradually became far more than that. Father succeeded in interesting Chinese universities and colleges in natural history courses and biological research. And we children were able to add a great deal to the knowledge of an untouched part of the world. Thousands of specimens went from the Coast of Fukien to the museums of America and Great Britain. As the collections grew, new species were found, some being of great importance in understanding the development of life on this planet. A grasshopper I collected on the slopes of Kuliang above Foochow proved to be of the same species as is found in the southwestern United States, thus letting one more tiny ray of light into the dark mystery of Asia's past relationship to North America.

In Futsing, we discovered two new kinds of birds; and there are a number of snakes, bats, and insects that bear the Latin "caldwellii" as a part of their scientific names. In the Museum of Natural History in New York there are thousands of specimens collected by Father, Da Da, Morris, and myself. Some of the finest examples of Asiatic big game fell before Father's gun. Most of our collections were donated to the institutions, but occasionally we were paid. The first money I ever earned was paid me by a British scientist for helping him gather grasshoppers, bugs, snakes, and lizards. I was seven at the time.

Father and I wrote and published a little paper-bound book called "Birds of the Lower Min Valley." It was such a success that we started work on a larger, more ambitious volume. I did most of the writing, using Father's meticulous notes of nearly thirty years. We spent many days and nights accumulating data on feeding and nesting habits. The book was finished and published when I was seventeen, a junior in high school. "South China Birds" was its title, and it was truly a family enterprise. Father and I did the research and writing; Morris was the photographer; and Muriel wrote the stories and legends and added color and flavor to its pages.

I sometimes blush when I re-read my first literary venture. The writing is not of the best, and here and there we made mistakes in scientific fact. But even today "South China Birds" is one of the most popular reference books for those interested in Far Eastern ornithology. Copies are still to be found in many American libraries. Above all, "South China Birds" provided the Chinese with much of the needed incentive for making accurate and scientific studies of their own.

Father also became an expert on the porcelain of the

Sung dynasty. His collection of Sung bowls is among the best.

We also wrote a book on the butterflies of China. It was to be beautifully illustrated with paintings made by a talented young Chinese artist who lived with us for several summers. Unfortunately, the cost of color reproductions is so great that this book has never been published. But we still preserve the manuscript and paintings among our family treasures.

Our exploits brought travellers, explorers, and scientists to our door. While we were living in Nanping on the Upper Min, Roy Chapman Andrews, who had discovered the dinosaur eggs in the Gobi dessert, made our home his headquarters during an expedition into the Fukien mountains. He urged Father to give up missionary work and join the staff of the American Museum of Natural History. It must have been a very great temptation. The salary was more than any missionary could ever hope to make. But father remembered his Promise.

He did, however, agree to accompany Mr. Andrews on an expedition into Mongolia. He obtained a three month leave of absence from the Methodist Mission and spent an exciting time among North China's wild mountains and along the edges of the Gobi desert. There he collected specimens for the American Museum's exhibits, one of them being the world's record Big Horn sheep.

Our hunting as well as our collecting consumed a great deal of hard-to-get shot-gun ammunition. For birds and small mammals are often collected with a shot gun, using very small shot. But fortunately Father, his brothers, and a sportsman dentist in Johnson City, Tennessee, had been faced with the same problem back in the 1890's. Working together, they had "invented" a very superior grade of almost smokeless powder. The inventors did very well with the powder, contracting to make shells for a Johnson City hardware store.

When Father went to China he gave us his financial interest in the powder, but took the formula with him. It was fortunate that he did so. It enabled us to load our own shells and saved much money, though occasionally it caused some trouble. The process was simple, but unless the ingredients were measured very carefully, the load could be too powerful or far from smokeless.

One day while pheasant hunting with Uncle Ernest Father shot a pheasant, but a few pellets also hit a farmer working in a rice paddy far below him.

Very quickly a mob gathered. A farmer attacked Uncle Ernest with a hoe. Father jumped the farmer and soon the situation was getting far out of control. Fortunately, a long-robed scholar came by at the crucial moment, a lengthy negotiation began, and the wounded farmer was sent to Foochow with a note addressed to Dr. Lacy, asking that all his medical expenses be paid. The original price of $100 per shot was compromised; the man received $1 each.

Soon after this unfortunate episode an English businessman heard of Father's powder and came to Fukien to investigate. He was very much interested in the commercial possibilities. Father made up a batch of powder for him and off he went to Peking. He sold the formula to Yuan Shi Kai, China's ruler at that time, and came back to Fukien with papers for Father's signature. Father was agreeable to the scheme, as he planned to put any royalties he received into church work. However, Yuan Shi Kai's government came to an abrupt end, before China's soldiers could be equipped with Caldwell powder.

In the days of uncertainty that followed change in government the formula got into the hands of Shanghai businessmen. These men began to manufacture the powder under the trade name "Wreck-a-Rock," and for years it was used as blasting powder in most of the construction jobs of Central China.

We continued to use the powder for our hunting and collecting, all of us becoming proficient in making it and in loading our shells. Many an evening Da Da, Father, Morris, and I would sit around the dining room table, busily preparing ammunition for the next day's hunt. And when a big load was needed for a well digging job or for blasting rock in a new church foundation, it could be whipped up very quickly.

I have personal knowledge that this powder was very effective in closing gates, also. Morris produced a batch one day, set up a target on the compound gate, and began testing. Mother arrived to investigate the shooting and was shocked to find good clean holes clear through the heavy boards of the Gate. She fully expected to find the alley outside piled high with corpses, and refused to allow the gate to be opened for several hours.

Birds, butterflies, animals, and fish—these brought us much enjoyment, a little money, and a measure of fame. But Father's interest in the out-of-doors had other, far more important aspects.

China had no Department of Agriculture, no county agricultural agents to help farmers solve their problems. There were no experiment stations to develop better crops, to plot against blights and insect pests. For many years the missionaries provided the Chinese farmer with the only help available in facing his serious problems.

Father had always been interested in bees. As a boy in Tennessee he had tracked down wild bee hives and had become an expert apiarist. Now he found wild honey bees in China. A few farmers raised bees, but the honey production was not what it could or should be. Father tackled the problem in his typical, thorough way. He sent home for some Italian Queens, which came all the way to China by boat, long before planes crossed the Pacific. He began breeding experiments which resulted in a new strain of bees, producing more honey than the native bees had ever produced. He also imported Rhode Island Red chickens to encourage greater egg production; and I can remember the scores of people who beat a path to our door asking for the seed of the new cabbage Father had imported.

But most vividly I remember what happened in connection with that wonderful Chinese fruit, the Lichee

Nut. Many Americans are familiar with the dried nuts, but few have ever tasted the fresh fruit. The Lichees, the Bee Ba, the Leng Eng are the finest fruits of the China Coast, and they brought in a large share of the farmer's cash.

One year the Lichee crop about Futsing showed signs of failing. By the next season, the loss was more pronounced and a wave of fear swept through the countryside. The disaster was, of course, attributed to the anger of some devil or god. Temples were visited, priests consulted, offerings made. But still the fruit withered on the bough.

Father and Claude Kellogg, Methodist agricultural missionary, decided to investigate. They visited scores of orchards, climbed scores of trees, and quickly discovered the source of the trouble.

Bugs, known to most American children as the common stink bug, had infested the trees. They were eating away the foliage, blossoms, and buds, and the trees were slowly dying.

The farmers were told what was happening, but apathy and superstition deafened their ears. There are so many bugs, beetles, and vermin in a Chinese farmer's life that the little stink bug had never been noticed. Many farmers maintained that no such bug existed.

The two missionaries, to prove their case, conducted an experiment. The ground under several fruit trees was spread with white sheets. While the crowds watched skeptically, Father climbed the trees and shook the branches with vigor. Down came a torrent of black bugs till the sheets were darkened.

To prove their point further, Kellog and Father offered to pay the children a copper for each bug brought in. Many bugs came in and many a copper went out. But the trees were kept free of stink bugs and produced the usual fine crops. By the following season, shaking stink bugs out of trees had become common practice, and the Lichee orchards were saved.

There were mountains we never had time to explore, mysteries we could not solve. I remember one Christmas time, when we had the rare treat of a snowfall. Da Da came rushing into the compound.

"The snow fish are here, the snow fish are here."

We followed Father to the market place, then on to the river's bank. There were hundreds of beautiful fish in the market. In the river fishermen were netting more fish, some weighing as much as ten pounds. Father had never seen such a fish before. To all his questions he got the same answer.

"It's the snow fish. We never catch them unless it snows. We never even see the fish at other times."

For years we searched for the answer to this mystery, for the waters in which the fish lived when it did not snow. Clifford Pope, famous naturalist of the American Museum of Natural History joined the search. He fished with poison, and with dynamite. His efforts brought up hundreds of other fish, of other species. But we never saw another snow fish, for it never snowed again. The old

fishermen of the Min had seen the fish a dozen times perhaps. But only when there is snow does the fish come to
the surface, only then is it ever taken in the nets.

Even Father's tiger hunting worked for the Glory of
God, leading to the scientific knowledge needed for
stamping out one of the most dreadful diseases of the
coast, a variety of schistomiasis known to the Chinese as
"big belly illness." A tiny parasite enters the body and
eventually produces huge abdominal swelling. Death is
almost inevitable. The parasite is a tiny fluke—but no one
knew how it entered the body or from whence it came.

Father had sent the Lister Institute in Shanghai the
lungs and other internal organs of tigers he had shot.
Researchers at the Institute were surprised to find the
same fluke infecting the lungs of tigers that infected human beings. It was the exact clue needed to trace down
the source of infection. For the tiger feeds upon the little mongoose which in turn feeds on the tiny fresh water
shrimp that abound in the rice paddies. It was the shrimp
that were host of the fluke. And since Chinese country
folk love the shrimp, sending the smallest children to
spend all day wading about the rice fields to collect them,
small wonder they became infected.

There are no tigers to hunt in Tennessee. There is no
scientific research needing the attention of a Methodist
ex-missionary. Retired and nearing eighty, Father has
been forced to direct his energy into other and quieter
channels. Today he is one of Tennessee's best trout fish-

ermen, and many a mountain farmer has rubbed his eyes in amazement to see a sturdy, white-haired angler wading down a turbulent mountain stream. At home in Nashville, he tends his other field of interest, a magnificent wild flower garden, augmented by each fishing trip. For the creel comes home with more flowers than fish. There are lovely trillium, lady's slippers, hepatica, orange fringed orchis, and birds' feet violets growing in such profusion that the passersby, even in cars, pause to behold and go away refreshed.

SCHOOL DAYS

THERE were many British missionaries along the China Coast. But there were few British children for us to know or play with, for British parents sent their children home to England when they came to school age, to see them only during furlough periods which fall five to seven years apart. Few American parents will suffer these long separations, which meant the education of American children was handled quite differently. We had our mothers; a correspondence school in far away Baltimore, Maryland; and finally the big American boarding school in Shanghai.

Whether we lived in Foochow, Nanping, or Futsing, we were actually students of the Calvert School in Baltimore. Our names were enrolled there as much as the names of any students living in the city.

The story is told that Calvert got its start as a correspondence school during a long period of epidemic illness (mumps—or was it measles?) in Baltimore. Schools were closed, and so the Calvert staff developed home study courses as a substitute. Now the tail wags the dog and there are thousands of Calvert extension students all over the world. Before Calvert School days the wives of Americans overseas had been teaching their children themselves with whatever books they could scrape together, with whatever methods they could devise.

The Calvert School was to us—and still is to some five thousand children on every continent—far more than a correspondence course. The School provided Mother with books and with instruction sheets. Our work was submitted to Baltimore for review, for grading, and for personal reports to us and advice to her. We did not officially graduate from one grade to another until word came from Baltimore. Of course, a very great deal depended on the mothers. I suspect the fact that none of the young Caldwells ever did very well in arithmetic can be traced to Mother's dislike for the subject.

School days were interesting days, and although there was a hiatus here and there, our educational experience was rich in many ways. The Calvert Courses provide for a half day's work; so all of us, Mother and children, had our afternoons free to collect birds' eggs, to go hunting, to enjoy each other. Sometimes, depending on where we were stationed, there would just be little Caldwells in "school" together. At one time Mother had five of us enrolled at Calvert in five different grades. At other stations there might be several missionary families and the mothers would cooperate. The children would go to school together, each mother handling a preferred grade.

My own most vivid memory of Calvert School days is of the exercises at my graduation from the third grade. We were living in Nanping. I had a little classmate, Louise Bankhardt, just my age. The Calvert Instruction Book said the graduation exercises must include putting on a play, "Little Bo Peep." The props needed included hay for Bo Peep to rest upon, so Louise and I went forth with a sickle to cut grass. The large awkward Chinese implement I was using slipped and cut a deep and bloody gash in Louise's arm. Today, thirty years later, the scar is still there.

As the American missionary enterprise in Asia increased in scope, as more and more children too old for Calvert came to the Mission stations, American high schools were established. There was one in North China, one in Seoul, Korea, one in Pyongyang, Korea (which my wife, the daughter of missionaries to Korea, attended when she had finished *her* Calvert course), and two in the mountains of central China. But *the* American School of Asia was the Shanghai American School, known as SAS to the thousands of Americans who attended it. Shanghai American School continued for nearly fifty years, through civil wars and revolutions. It tried to keep its doors open after the Communists took over Shanghai in 1949, and was successful for a short time. But the Peoples' Republic put the school out of business by a method often used with foreign enterprises. It levied back taxes in such enormous amounts that payment was impossible and the institution was confiscated by the State for failure to pay. The physical plant still stands in Shanghai, but is now used for Communist enlightenment of Chinese youth.

The great day of our young lives was the day when we "went away" to high school. It was the first separation from home and parents, and for most of us the first real contact with numerous other young Americans of our age. For us all, SAS was a wonderful experience, dreamed about for years in advance, looked forward to and yet feared. It meant life in the metropolitan atmosphere of one of the world's most glamorous cities. It also meant long absences from home, and travel alone.

Foochow lies nearly 500 miles south of Shanghai, and there were then no roads along the coast. Travel to and from School was by coastal steamer, and the boats were some of the smallest and dirtiest in the world. The trip took as little as thirty hours or as much as a week. Occasionally the ships were captured by the pirates that operated out of Bias Bay, south of Foochow. There was a period when piracy reached such a pitch that the ship's bridge, officers' quarters, and first class space were barricaded behind iron grills and the officers went armed. The pirates usually came aboard in port, as steerage or deck passengers. At a prearranged point they would take over and steer the ship to some isolated cove where confederates would loot, kill, and kidnap for ransom. So our journeys to SAS were full of adventure for the children and anxiety for the parents.

There were several steamship lines that touched at Pagoda Anchorage, but only one had a regular schedule. This was the Japanese line running from Formosa to Shanghai and on to the north. Other ships came and went as passengers signed up and cargoes piled up. An announcement would be posted throughout Foochow that the *S. S. Ningshin* or the *S. S. Hsinchi* was scheduled to sail for Shanghai with the tide on a certain day. Our parents would hire a junk or a launch and off we'd go downstream the twelve miles to Pagoda Anchorage.

There would normally be long, inexplicable delays while we young ones made merry on shipboard. By the time all the missionary children had been funneled into the port from the up-river mission stations, from Futsing, Hingwha, and Sienyu down the coast, there would be as many as thirty of us.

Traveling without chaperones, we had a gay time and I'm sure made life miserable for the officers and crew—in fact, there came a dark age when one of the ships refused to book passage for the SAS crowd. However, our pranks were seldom of a serious nature. The worst *I* ever did was on board the *Seikyo Maru*, a Japanese ship, when I took a bath and then let out the fresh water. The steward was furious. That one tubful was expected to be the bath water for all the passengers for the whole trip.

The irregularities of ships' sailings were a great help

in wangling ourselves extra vacation days at both ends. At
school one boy from each China coast port would be
selected "trip manager" for Christmas vacations or end-
of-school departures from Shanghai. He would check
sailings and make bookings for all the boys and girls
headed for his home port—whether it was Foochow,
Amoy, or Swatow. He was expected to find—and usually
did find—that the only ship which would get us home
for Christmas sailed a week or so before school let out.
At the other end of the line, our parents did a bit of similar
conniving to keep us with them longer. The two weeks
Christmas vacation had a way of becoming a three or
four week holiday.

One fall, Ed Gillette, whose Father ran a little Congregational Mission Hospital at Pagoda Anchorage, decided to go to school in a sailboat; for he had become
friendly with a man who owned one. The two set sail
well before school opening in September under a cloud
of dire predictions from some of the other parents.

The China Sea was exceptionally calm that fall. Ed and
his companion were "lost" among the islands for nearly
a month for lack of wind. Frantic cables were being sent
to cable stations and lighthouses along the coast seeking
reports of when and where they had been sighted last.
The little boat finally made the mouth of the Yangtse,
and Ed appeared at School, thin, tanned, and a hero.

But even without the thrills of a month at sea in a sailing craft, we did have unforgettable experiences. Some of
us were almost pirated; we all rode through typhoons;

our ships ran aground. I made the China Coast trip from Pagoda Anchorage to Shanghai twenty-seven times, in every shape and condition of ship from Jardine-Mathieson ocean liners to Chinese tramp steamers.

The Shanghai American School was similar in every respect to an accredited American school. It was under the supervision of a Board of Directors, had an American principal, and American teachers. We had a football team (with limited competition—the big game being with a U. S. Marine team on Thanksgiving Day), baseball, tennis, basketball, and track teams. We were not all missionary offspring. Of the average enrollment of 500, perhaps half were day students from the Shanghai area. Many of these were from the families of American businessmen. From up and down the coast came the children of Standard Oil, of sea captains and lighthouse keepers. One of my earliest passions was for the daughter of a lighthouse keeper off Amoy. She was a beautiful Eurasian girl, blending Japanese, Chinese, Scotch, American, and other bloods. Next came Sophie Novitska, daughter of a refugee Polish Count.

In its early days, SAS was rather strait-laced. Smoking was punished by immediate expulsion. Dancing was forbidden. The girl who kissed and was discovered was definitely fallen. But as the years passed, the missionary viewpoint broadened somewhat—before I graduated, we had **many** socials! But unchaperoned dates were *never* permitted. The big event was escorting a girl to the movies. To reduce the cost of the chaperone's ticket and the taxi, three couples would join forces; and the popular chaperones were those who said they preferred to sit alone.

For many of us the transition from Calvert School to SAS was painful. At home, American playmates were few and far between, while in Shanghai we were thrown with hundreds of other American boys and girls. And the way of life of the big city was sharply different from that of the lonely coastal mission stations.

I shall never forget my own first great crisis. At home we were taught to say our prayers, kneeling beside the bed; each morning the family and servants had a short morning prayer service. The night prayers had become almost second nature to me. The first night in the Boys' Dormitory, in a room with three other boys, I was faced with the fact that they were not "kneelers." One of my roommates was a Jewish boy, another from a Standard Oil family, the third from a missionary family in Canton evidently more liberal than mine. I was anxious to make good with my new friends. I could not face the action that would make me different.

I am afraid that my faith did not stand up that night. I could not bring myself to do what the others were not doing. Ashamed, I crept into bed. After "lights out" I slipped out again and said my prayers. Unfortunately, Standard Oil saw me and twitted me. The result was a fight, the noise roused the dormitory supervisor, and we both received demerits. Worse still, the fracas was the beginning of an enmity between us. After several days the other boys decided that Bob and I should fight it out in a ring, with gloves. I had never set eyes on boxing gloves. In fact, I had never had a fight in my life. I had no idea how to use my fists. I was scared to death and was ignominiously defeated. My religious upbringing also suffered an eclipse, and henceforth, I said my prayers in bed, though, I think, a little longer and more fervently.

During our years on the China Coast, five Caldwells attended SAS. We received a remarkably good education. My oldest brother, Oliver, gained fame for his athletic prowess. My sister, Muriel, was a good student who in later years came back to teach at SAS herself. There she met John Pilley, a missionary's son who had graduated from SAS and was teaching there. They were married in 1932, uniting a pioneer missionary family from the South China Coast with one from Central China. And Morris, my younger brother, distinguished himself by a number of escapades including a fight with a French policeman.

SAS was located in the Old French Concession of Shanghai. We technically lived under French law. Morris and two other boys, walking about one Saturday night, decided to use stones to practice their marksmanship on the street lights. The first shot was a bulls-eye. The police came running and the boys went running. It ended in a free-for-all, with fists, in a cabbage patch. Morris was not unhappy about the explosion at school. Hitting a large Frenchman on the head with an equally large cabbage was at least a moral victory.

My own fame in the Shanghai American School rested only on the fact that I had become co-author of a book on birds at the age of seventeen, and that I managed to fall over a 150 foot waterfall and live. The accident cut short my own SAS days. I was in and out of the school, but actually spent only two and a half years there, finally graduating because the faculty helped me. On graduation day I was short of credits, but the principal was an understanding man and allowed me to take part in the Commencement exercises with my classmates. I received a be-ribboned roll of blank paper in lieu of my diploma. Then I went home to Foochow and before sailing for America and the final big adventure of college, SAS allowed me to study a specially set-up course in "Advanced Bible." I did the required reading, wrote my reports, and on the way to America in August, picked up my diploma all properly filled in.

The two and a half years at SAS were full years. I was unable to follow in Oliver's athletic footsteps, and could not even match my younger brother, Morris, but I did make the tennis team. I also became editor of the school paper and secretary of the Dorm Council.

The Council was in charge of discipline, meting out punishment for minor offenses. The punishment consisted of demerits and rear-end paddlings with a very large paddle. A sufficient number of demerits could mean suspension or expulsion. In my official position, I had the privilege of sitting in judgment over Morris on several occasions, and also of wielding the paddle.

Morris seemed to have an infinite capacity for getting into trouble and getting caught at it. My own conduct was not of the best, but I was more clever in escaping detection.

Now it can be told that it was I who managed to hoist a huge ash can to the top of the flag pole, shinny up the pole and fasten the rope so well that it was necessary to call the French Fire Department in order to remove the can and again raise our flag.

For some reason I could never understand, ringing the fire alarm bell in the School quadrangle ranked with smoking and stealing as a crime deserving suspension. It made the ringing of the bell a real challenge! We wracked our brains to think of new methods of doing it and getting away with it. We tried tying a long string to the clapper, the string leading up to our third floor dormitory, then when all was quiet after "lights out" we pulled the string vigorously and broke it off, which left no possible clue. I accomplished this trick several times and was not apprehended. Once, when I was ill with mumps and confined to the sick bay, the bell was rung. The sick bay was located on the ground floor of the Girls' dormitory not far from the bell. I was shocked when the principal took it for granted that I had committed the crime. I was saved only by the confession of the real culprit.

There were friendships at SAS that have lasted through the years. Father's reputation as a tiger hunter followed us to Shanghai and we were invited to hunt with boys who lived nearby. Dr. J. R. Snell, one of China's most famous missionary surgeons, lived at Soochow, fifty miles from Shanghai by rail. Raymond Snell, his son, and I became great friends, and we often organized hunting trips with our classmates into the Soochow Hills and the country around the Tai Hu—the Great Lake of China—where dog-sized river deer abounded. On Saturdays or short holidays (we did not hunt on Sundays) we would take a train to Soochow and there hire a houseboat. After traveling by canal overnight, we would in the morning be in the center of the hill and lake country. Ray and I became the great hunters of SAS and gained much face by occasionally bringing enough venison to feed the whole school.

Ray, Lincoln Brownell (who comes of a Canton missionary family, and is now a successful New York lawyer), and I had been reading with interest a series of articles on Chiang Kai Shek's new army. It claimed that the soldier of new China was the toughest in the world and could outwalk the soldier of any country in the world. Such a positive assertion, so unproved, roused our patriotic instincts. We decided to prove that Americans could walk as far as a Chinese any day. Ray's home was in Soochow, fifty-four miles from Shanghai by rail. We decided to walk it in one day. The Chinese soldier's record was said to be fifty miles.

We went into several strenuous weeks of training for our walkathon in Shanghai's suburbs, and made quite a study of foods which would produce the greatest energy. When we felt sufficiently fit, we set the date. We were up and on our way by four in the morning, without the knowledge of school or parents, and almost ran the several lonely and dangerous miles from SAS to Shanghai's North Station. The streets of the city were very poorly patrolled at that hour and very dimly lit. I was badly frightened at the outset when we were accosted on the Tibet Road by numbers of prostitutes. I had never seen anything like it.

North Station was closed up tight as a drum. We scaled a wall into the rail yards and started westward up the tracks. Anyone trying for a distance record on foot should know better than to select a railroad bed to walk on. The ties were too far apart to use as stepping stones. It was up and down, up and down for hours, cinders in our shoes and painful bruises. Near the ancient city of Quinsan we were taken into custody by two unfriendly bayonet-waving soldiers who conducted us to a nearby Army post where we were accused of being Russian spies. Ray was very good in the Shanghai dialect and we were finally released, but we had lost a lot of time.

Further up the track, where the railroad crosses the Grand Canal, we were invited aboard a luxurious British-owned houseboat and given a cold drink. Later we bathed in the canal.

At the forty-fourth mile stone I broke down. In stepping off a tie I wrenched my knee and had to call it quits. I was able to hobble to a nearby station, and took the next train to Soochow. I had walked forty-four miles in thirteen hours. Ray and Lincoln continued, and reached Soochow at nine o'clock that night. They had walked over fifty-five miles that day in the excellent time of seventeen hours. We felt we had vindicated American manhood.

Shanghai school days were rich days in many ways, but there were important things we did not learn, knowledge which should have been imparted but was not. We studied the things American children studied: algebra, English, Latin, and French, ancient and modern history. The reputation of the school was such that its graduates could gain ready admission to the best American colleges and universities. But our elders had little sense of the importance of the country we were living in, of the people we lived among. It was only during my last years that Chinese history was taught, and then only as an elective. There was no course in the rich culture of our host country. It was even later that the Chinese language was added to the curriculum, but still not as a required subject.

SAS also failed in a considerable degree to equip us for the life that lay ahead in America. Missionary children lead lives that are fraught with difficult psychological problems. In Futsing there were tigers, bandits, wars, and rumors of wars. There was beauty, but there were also the rough facts of life everywhere in sight, life at its coarsest. In my memory there was not a single word of sex education in my childhood or in the childhood of any of the missionary children I knew. From this exciting but actually sheltered life, we passed to the life of the Shanghai American School in a cosmopolitan city of 4,000,000 people.

Shanghai has always had one of the largest prostitute populations in the world. Nanking Road from the Race track to the Bund teemed with them and their procurers. A fair share of the rickshaw coolies engaged in pandering for extra cash. Yet in such an environment we were given a single booklet on sex that was written in such a way and couched in such terms that it was not sex education at all and undoubtedly caused lifelong problems for some of us.

Nor did the lack of worldly education, the lack of understanding of the vices and supposed vices of the world, prepare us for the next great step—going to America. We never spoke of "going home," because China was home to us. Each year the graduates of SAS would leave Shanghai in August or early September for the new and often very lonely life ahead. The trip across the Pacific or the long way 'round by Suez would be fun because there were always many friends traveling together. Then when we arrived in San Francisco, Seattle, or New York, there would be the excitement of a long train trip alone, usually followed by short visits with aunts and uncles, brothers or sisters. And after that came the cold plunge into the utter strangeness of an American college campus. New temptations faced us, and our innocent childhood, our bewildered days at SAS, had not quite prepared us for what we faced.

My first year in college was the loneliest and most

frightening period of my life. I know too of missionary sons and daughters who failed to take this great transition in their stride. They became twisted, mentally and spiritually. Perhaps this is the basis of the old saying that there is no one wilder than a minister's son. There could be some truth in it, and good reason.

But in spite of the loneliness and occasional heartache, in spite of the lingering sense of insecurity and the necessity for most of us to work hard to pay for our education, China Coast background was far more good than evil. Though a few were warped, there are those who have succeeded beyond measure. Educators, writers, clergymen, and lawyers have been born of China Coast families. There are the Burke brothers: Jim is now a well-known writer; Gordon is high in the diplomatic service. Faith Baldwin's Grandfather arrived at Pagoda Anchorage in 1859. Paul Hutchison is a distinguished editor. Kesser, Dana, and Francis Nance, sons of a pioneer missionary doctor, are all doctors. There is Dr. Louis Alvarez, the physicist. There are families like the Lacy's who have had three generations of service as missionaries, not only in China, but throughout the world.

With all its failings, the life and education that the China Coast gave us can never be forgotten. For we were in a sense the children of the last American pioneers. Our parents had no Indians to fight, but they fought superstition, idolatry, even hatred instead. Time will show, I feel sure, that their sacrifices were not in vain.

6

_{wwwwwwwwwwwwwwww}

BANDITS

BANDITS, both of the land and the sea, shared top
honors with tigers on the China Coast of my
boyhood. Indeed, at times the bandits even shared
living quarters with their four-legged colleagues in the
mountain recesses of Fukien. My earliest memories are of
bandit talk among the servants, stories of the terrible
atrocities committed by the dreaded "tu-peis." I remember the sensation in the American community when Jay
Dinsmore, an American lumber merchant, was killed in
the mountains above Nanping. There was the kidnap-
ping of two missionary ladies for ransom, with a bloody
finger of one of the ladies enclosed with the ransom
note. Mother was once captured and held for four hours.
John Pilley, my brother-in-law, suffered the indignity of

having his pants taken away by bandits and walking ten pantless miles home. Scores of American missionary families had similar experiences. Generally there was no physical harm done.

Except for a brief period when Chiang Kai Shek was at the height of his power, there have been bandits among the Fukien hills and pirates along the coast. At times they have been so active that they have disrupted the economic life of the coast, and made travel nearly impossible. Banditry had its roots in economic conditions, in misrule, in the very nature of the Fukienese. For centuries the inhabitants of Fukien Province have been the non-conformists, the adventurers of China. As early as the tenth century, the high-powered junks from Fukien reached the Arabian Sea. For generations Fukienese have emigrated, and today are the business heart of Malaya, Borneo, Indo-China, and Indonesia. One cannot walk the streets of many a South Asian or Indonesian city without hearing the Foochow, or some other Fukienese dialect.

As non-conformists, the Fukienese have often sat on the fence in civil wars; or fought for years against an alien enemy; or cast their lots unpredictably from one side to the other; or joined one of the bandit or pirate gangs that have roamed the hills and seas since the time of Koxinga. During the Revolution of 1911-12 which ended the rule of the Emperors, the Fukien Government, instead of immediately joining the Revolution, took neither side for awhile. Fukien postage stamps were overprinted in Chinese with the characters "For the Present Neutral,"

until the leaders decided which way to go. The stamps
are rare collectors' items today.

In the years that followed the Revolution, there was a
succession of weak rulers in China. There were hordes of
soldiers roaming the country, with allegiance to the Government, or to the greedy war lords, or to no one at all.
They were undisciplined, often cruel, and followed the
time honored custom of looting and living off the land.
Cruelty begets cruelty, and the sturdy Fukienese fought
back. Any act of resistance brought cruel retaliation
which, in turn, forced the peasants into the mountains
where the change from citizen to bandit came easily.
Soon the Fukien mountains were full of bona fide bandits, soldier-bandits, and peasant-bandits. It was unsafe
to travel the mountain paths or the river roads.

Our family landed squarely in the midst of bandit
country when Father was assigned to work a term in
Nanping.

There were men of good will in the Chinese Government who wanted an end to banditry; there were bandits
who were anxious to return to their ancestral fields, who
were sick of killing and looting. The problem was to get
the two groups together, to establish a climate in which
negotiations could be completed so that peace might
come back to the hills.

Chinese distrusted Chinese. Past negotiations had too
often ended in treachery. What could be better than to
find an American to hold the all important position of
middle man? And what more natural than to turn to a
beloved and admired missionary?

Father seemed to be the logical man. The bandits admired him for his hunting exploits which were the talk of the land. The Government respected him for his integrity and good works. His parish converts loved him as a man of God. So Father was officially asked to become Bandit Pacification Commissioner of Fukien, mediator in negotiations to bring an end to war and bloodshed.

The American Consul in Foochow was shocked when he heard of the Government request. He warned Father that no American should interfere in the internal affairs of the Chinese. If they wanted to go about killing and robbing each other, that was their business. Father took a somewhat different view of the matter. To him, this was another opportunity to do the Lord's work. In spite of dire warnings that he would lose the protection afforded him by his American citizenship if he went ahead, Father plunged into his new task, and kept at it until the day he left China.

Father returned from his visit to the Consul and discussed the matter with Mother.

"Well, Harry," Mother said. "If you think you can really help people I suppose you should go ahead. But I wonder if you are not taking on too much. How can you continue all your preaching, all your other extras and do this too?"

"I can do it," Father replied. "Even if I have to give up some other things. I certainly can give up butterflies and tigers. If a missionary cannot help in times like these he should go home."

To understand fully the difficulties of such negotiations, one must understand some of the peculiar situations and the rivalries of the Chinese war-lords of that period. The military were vying for honors, ready to resort to treachery and intrigue to outdo one another. A ranking general was secretly supplying a powerful bandit chief with arms and ammunition with which to fight other bandits, thus purchasing immunity for himself from that particular bandit. The Japanese added to the confusion by supplying arms to any bandit on the theory that a disrupted China would be easy prey.

The outbreak of banditry in the Yuki area in the mountains southwest of Foochow is illustrative of the beginning of similar troubles elsewhere. A severe famine struck there a few years after the Revolution. The suffering among the people was acute because of the rice shortage. But, as has always been true in China, while there was famine for the many, there was an abundance for the few. Living in one corner of the country was a wealthy land owner named Su Ek, whose bins were full of rice from a previous harvest. Su Ek was so moved by the suffering of his people that he discussed the matter of disposing of surplus rice with other wealthy land owners. It was agreed that Su Ek would be the first to open his bins to the famine stricken and would sell the rice to them at reasonable prices. This he did, until all his surplus was gone. Then when hungry farmers gathered around his empty bins, Su Ek told them to go to the house of another wealthy land owner not far distant. On reaching this house, the people met with a rude rebuff. They were told that the rice was available, but only at an outrageous price. Pleading was to no avail, and so the people helped themselves and left in payment the same amount they had been paying Su Ek.

The profiteering land owner disappeared. Everyone thought that he was in hiding to dodge the criticism heaped on him for his selfish behavior. But he was in Foochow making a deal with a General for an expedition into the Yuki area against the "bandits." One way to get ahead in the military was by producing a large number of bandit bodies. With no great difficulty the General worked up considerable enthusiasm for the project among his officers and enlisted men, since they were assured the bandits were unorganized and unprepared.

The name of the bandit chief, the exact location of the village, and even the houses, were supplied by the land owner. That bandit chief was Su Ek, the benefactor and friend of the people!

The General's forces swooped down on Su Ek's village, killing and capturing many innocent farmers. Su Ek himself escaped into the hills, and soon placards appeared in the market places offering a reward for him, dead or alive.

Many villagers used the opportunity to even up old scores. Everyone was secretly accusing his personal enemies of being "bandits." No one was safe. Blackmail became the order of the day. Those with money and rice suffered first and suffered most. Scores of people, fearing they would be denounced, blackmailed, or executed, fled to the hills and rallied around Su Ek. Thus a bandit chief was born.

Father took a trip up the Yuki River soon after the mess began. I was "let out" of school to accompany him. It was a lovely and exciting trip for a small boy. We traveled down the Min River from Nanping in a small sampan, flying the American flag for protection against bandits and soldiers. Those were the days when the Stars and Stripes still afforded some protection.

The Min River is a wild flowing stream in its upper reaches, with rapids and whirlpools every few miles. It is great sport to shoot the rapids, or to stop and collect butterflies on some flower-covered sandpit or island. At night we made camp in time to allow for a brief hunt or a collecting foray.

Thirty miles below Nanping the Yuki River flows in from the South. We pushed and poled up toward Yuki City. And it was just below Yuki City we saw a terrible sight, one that became indelibly impressed on my child's mind.

First came a boatload of soldiers guarding a group of farmers, their arms bound tightly behind their backs. To me they differed in no way from the thousands of peasants we had passed on the river banks. But they were on their way to Foochow for trial as bandits, exhibition and execution. A few hundred yards up the river, such a "trial" had just taken place. There on the sandy shore lay the bloody bodies of other peasants, just executed in the manner of Old China, by beheading. Among the bodies was the head of what seemed to have been a boy, still smiling, while not far off was the little trunk that matched the head. Nearby was the blood-smeared body of a man, still alive and groaning with pain. A great gaping wound all but severed his neck, but he was conscious. No man dared to extend him a helping hand, or even offer a drink of water. The soldiers were probably forcing him to live and suffer, trusting some relative would offer them a few dollars to end his misery. Father knelt by the man's side and heard his story. It seemed that in order to settle a clan feud of long standing, members of a rival clan had secretly informed the military that he had been seen buying straw hats for the bandits. That was all that was necessary, and the man paid the price, going the way of thousands of his kind.

Father was shocked and furious. That night he was to preach in the Yuki Church. He scrapped his prepared sermon and preached instead of the evil that had befallen the city. He declared that if the Gospel of Christ could not stop such butchery, he would leave China. It was a bold and daring thing to do, and when he uttered his challenge Father had no idea how he would go about making it good. But events, with perhaps a helping hand from the Lord, gave him his opportunity. His sermon was talked about everywhere, and bandit emissaries soon called on him to urge him to act as a conciliator.

Several years earlier Father had entertained the vice-Speaker of the Peking Parliament. A friendship had grown up between them. Now Father got in touch with his old friend and reported the situation. Letters and telegrams were exchanged. Soon there came an official request from the Governor of Fukien, and with it credentials which placed absolute power in Father's hands as the official representative of the Chinese Government in dealing with bandits. This was a bit more than he had bargained for. Originally he had intended only to use his good offices as a missionary to call the attention of a friend and member of Parliament to the crimes being committed. But after his sermon in Yuki City, he felt he could not retreat. In fact, he felt the Lord had intervened to make him His servant and messenger.

In spite of the American Consul's objections Father went ahead. Whatever Mother said about all this, I hardly imagine she was very pleased with the arrangement. But from that day until he left China nearly a quarter of a century later, Father was involved not only with bandits, but later with the pirates of the Futsing Coast. He handled kidnappings and various other extra-legal affairs where a solution without loss of face was needed.

Though Father had authority from both sides to do what he thought best to bring about an amicable settlement, his first problem was how to proceed without an unfavorable reaction on the part of the Church, always his first concern. Should there be treachery on either side, the Church would suffer. If, on the other hand, it became generally known that he was acting with such full authority, there might be too many converts at the church door. Father was always very sensitive to the oft-repeated charge that many Chinese became Christians for the sake of prestige, protection, or better jobs. He decided to all but close the church membership, making enrollment next to impossible. Then he decreed that no reformed bandit could become a Christian under any circumstances for the period of a full year. To make his position doubly sure he refused to permit either the bandit chiefs or the Chinese government to pay his traveling expenses.

I was very young when the bandits first came into our lives, and had little understanding of the meaning of Father's many trips into the Yuki mountains. To convey the drama, the dangers, the accomplishments of that phase of his missionary work, Father must speak for himself. I quote from his own writings:

"Chief Ling selected as a meeting place a small village hanging on the almost perpendicular face of a chasm where a great notch had been cut through the high range of mountains. There was absolutely no approach other than by one winding path up the rugged mountain, then along the top of the range for miles. The road was plainly visible from almost any strategic point across the chasm. When the road reached a point about two miles from the lonely hamlet it suddenly dropped into the chasm and across the wild river which had created it. The strategy of the bandits' stronghold was very evident to me as soon as our guide pointed out the village from the distant mountain top, and I realized that they were taking absolutely no chance when they agreed to meet me at such a trysting place.

"I had with me a high military officer and special Deputy from the Tuchun in Foochow, my own interpreter, Da Da as cook, and a burden bearer. I could, of course, converse directly with the bandits, but because the military men from the north could not understand a word of the Foochow dialect, it was necessary to take along someone who could be ears for them to know all that I was saying. I had been instructed by the bandits not to bring any extra men, so I had previously sent in a list of those who would be in my party. It was pointed out to me that there was great danger of being fired upon if I took a greater number than I had designated.

"I learned later that the bandits had been informed by agents of the munitions dealers that I was taking along a lot of soldiers under the guise of personal servants and coolies, and that during the night these men would rise and attack the bandits. I soon realized the situation I faced, the tense feeling of suspicion on all sides. But once the interview started I must say that I have never had dealings with a more straightforward lot of men than these outlaws.

"I had no particular prestige among them other than that I was a missionary, and an American, but I resolved in the very beginning that I would permit nothing that would impair the confidence they were manifesting. I refrained from being so much as seen in conversation with any of my party except under conditions wholly above suspicion.

"Upon reaching the village overhanging the tumbling river, looking now like a silver thread among the dense growth of laurel and rhododendron in the depths of the canyon, I was led into a beautifully decorated room where a feast was spread. Everything seemed to be normal in the village. There was no one in sight that I could so much as suspect of being a bandit. One distinguished-looking man came forward and talked with us for a time, until he obviously became satisfied that everything was all right, whereupon he announced to me that the brigands had not yet arrived, but that he had been asked to entertain us. He said they would be unable to arrive from a far distant point until nine o'clock in the evening, but that we were to make ourselves at home in the village. At that very moment sharpshooters were watching our every movement.

"Although weary from my twenty-mile tramp over the rugged mountains I enjoyed the following hours studying their way of making paper from bamboo pulp. The interest I manifested in the industry and in the village life in general seemed to gain me the confidence of the villagers. Young men began to slip down through the bamboo groves behind the village as if in response to some signal. We talked of paper-making, of wild boar hunting, of tigers, of life in far away America. Finally, I began to talk of education, only to find that there had never been a school in the community. Yet there were a number of young men who could read well, and talk intelligently concerning many problems of the outside world. It developed that as boys, they had studied in a Christian day school in a distant town, and it was their knowledge of the Church and of missionaries that was responsible for the attitude of confidence in me I had thought emanated from their chief. For these young men *were* the bandits, and they were the very brains of the gang. It required brains to exist at all in the kind of life they were forced to live.

"During this first night with them I began to learn the true character of the men with whom I was dealing. I heard later that only a few days after my visit, and before the final details of the matter we had discussed were definitely agreed upon, one of the men who sat around the council chamber with me that night was stood against a tree and shot by his fellows because he had acted in a manner to bring them discredit. I learned of bandit discipline and justice, of the code which they must all follow.

"Upon being summoned to supper we were ushered again into the room we had first entered. The light from many lanterns made a wonderfully beautiful glow. I found a table spread with a more sumptious feast than one would ever expect to find in such an out-of-the-way place, or in such company. The chopsticks were of carved ivory, many of the dishes and utensils of rolled silver. I had never seen anything like it in the homes of the rich, and could not conceal my surprise at the lavish display.

"As we were being seated around the table with the usual haggling and argument as to who should have what seat, a man whispered in my ear, 'The Chief has done you a great honor in preparing such a feast.' I realized this

forcibly enough, but felt a keen disappointment because
no one who looked in the least like a bandit was seated
around the oval table. I found out later the bandits were
near at hand in sufficiently large numbers. It being my
first appearance among the outlaws, Chief Ling had been
cautioned by the other chiefs to play absolutely safe lest
another trap be sprung by the military. The eyes of at
least four bandit gangs were watching the whole show
from backstage, and there were enough men within ear-
shot to have cleaned up all the soldiers in the Province.

"Everything went off perfectly during the feast, which
was ordered according to the ways and usages of such
events. I was profoundly impressed by the etiquette of
the occasion, but nearly collapsed when an expression of
confidence of which I had often heard but never seen was
pulled off. I think it was about the twelfth course when
a large rooster, fairly swimming in delicious gravy and
covered with mushrooms, was brought in. As the platter
of fowl was placed in the center of the table, and before
any move had been made to dismember it, the man acting
as my host arose, and with great deliberation removed
the enormous comb from the bird's head. With an unused
pair of chopsticks he placed the comb on a silver tray.
Taking the tray in both hands he walked twice around
the table with the air of a priest about to do sacrifice to
the Gods, stopped the second time around at my left,
made a low bow, and with great dignity placed the tray
before me. Realizing the seriousness of the situation I rose
and made an equally low bow. I did not at the time un-

derstand the full significance of the ceremony. The man sitting at my right leaned over and whispered in my ear, 'You are crowned. This is the greatest token of confidence known among our people.'

"Anyway, the ice was certainly broken, for the several villagers seated around the table who had previously been silent, now freely began to discuss the whole bandit situation with me. They appeared to ignore the presence of the military men. The bandit chief's private secretary and others high in authority no longer tried to conceal their identities. With the "crowning" they had committed their lives into my hands unreservedly, and I began for the first time to understand what it meant to represent men of this character in a cause of this kind. For a few seconds I almost wished I was out of the whole thing, but on more sober reflection I realized that the undertaking was a great success as far as the bandits were concerned, and that my task was to safeguard the interests of these sturdy mountain people who trusted me so wholeheartedly.

"I well knew that if I did not act wisely there might be serious consequences. My first move would have to be made with very great care. What I did staggered the military men who had accompanied me, but it settled once and for all the character of the deliberations. I was assured by the interpreter, when we retired for a few minutes rest just before dawn, that I had absolutely settled the matter and that there would be no attempt at trickery on their part or on the part of those whom they represented.

"After the feast table had been cleared, Chief Ling and ten accompanying officers walked in and seated themselves. I made known my purpose in seeking an interview. I pointed out that the Tuchun, or military governor, in Foochow, had a spokesman in Mr. Chang; that the commander of the troops assigned to bandit control had General Wang; I enlarged on the fact that these men acted with the authority of those whom they represented. I then said that I wished to be the representative of the bandits, responsible to them for all that I did or agreed upon. I made it clear that I would stand firmly for fair play, would be myself responsible for the carrying out of all agreements. The spectacle of an American asking for the privilege of representing the bandits was something new to these people who had been driven into banditry because they had never before had a man to stand up for their rights and be heard. No further words were needed for *their* pledge of sincerity. And the military too became bound for they would lose great face if they double-crossed an American missionary.

"We had been seated around the table an hour or more, deliberating the terms of settlement as they were laid down one by one from each side, when suddenly every bandit at the table leaped to his feet at the hooting of an owl in the distance. They jammed the door in a fever of excitement. At first I failed to realize what had caused the commotion and remained calmly at my place. From where I sat I could look out across the deep chasm to the trail we had traveled in the afternoon. And on it, and fully three miles away, I saw a number of moving lights.

What they were, I have never learned, but the sharp eye of a bandit sentinel had spotted them at the first glimmer and the lonely call of an owl pierced the night. The signal had electrified the bandits, and every man was ready for fight or flight. It was an indication of the terrible tension of the hour.

"Without leaving my chair, and without showing the least apparent concern, I said 'Brothers, I have agreed to represent you in a faithful way in this important matter, and I mean to do it if you give me the opportunity; I am wholly responsible for what takes place. I bid you be in peace and return to your seats that we may continue the deliberations.'

"Straightway each bandit went back to his place. Only the look-out remained at the door and watched the movement of the lights. I was just as much interested in those lights as any man present, for not only the success of my mission, but my own life as well might be in the balance. I dared not show the least concern, however, lest there be a stampede into the hills. All night the mysterious lights haunted me, for there was no telling what some aspiring young officer might be up to. I was greatly relieved when I could see the tall bamboos waving in the dawn wind and there was an excuse for us to be up and about. My first night in the bandit stronghold was over, and the suspense relieved.

"The deliberations had been entirely successful. Arrangements had been made for the turning in of all guns and ammunition, the time and place of issuing pardons had been agreed upon. Of course General Wang was much elated, for he could report the success of the meeting to his superior, emphasizing what *his* efforts had accomplished. A promotion would undoubtedly be his reward.

"The bandits crowded around me like enthusiastic schoolboys, thanking me for the service I had rendered them, each eager to know when he could return to his home and family. As bandits they had terrified their enemies, and exacted a heavy toll from the soldiery in every conflict. They were now well armed and equipped for a better defense than ever before. Yet all were eager to quit the business. This was a moment of supreme happiness for several hundred outlaws who had been highwaymen for months, even years, but from no choice of their own.

"As we left the following morning, after a breakfast that equalled the feast of the evening before, the mountains and ravines echoed to the banging of fire crackers and the firing of small field pieces. I heard one man say to another 'Our cause is perfectly safe in the hands of that missionary, for he is an American.'

"Within a few days every condition agreed upon was met and one band of outlaws passed out of existence. Word was passed to other bandit chiefs and within a short time I found myself overwhelmed with unlimited requests for my services as a mediator."

As I re-read Father's bandit stories, I cannot help wondering how often in the world today we would find men like the bandit in the Chinese mountain village who said, "I trust the missionary, for he is an American." I am sure there are men still living on the China Coast who would say it. As long as that is so, and if we will act on it before it is too late, China is not lost to us.

7

wwwwwwwwwwwwww

OLIVER MEETS
THE BANDITS

T HE Chinese bandits were well organized, and
certain unwritten laws guide their operations.
Each band operated in a definite area, and it was
a serious breach of bandit etiquette and faith for one band
to poach in the territory of another. Death was the inevitable end for the bandits found guilty of this crime.
There was the law which made a person exempt from
further assessment after he had once paid ransom for
release. If he held a receipt from a bandit chief for payment of ransom, he could not be shaken down a second
time. Those bandits who refused to obey the "laws" were
known as "wild bandits" and if caught were summarily
executed.

Discipline was excellent. A village captured by bandits would within the hour have placards posted, giving the rules of occupation—rules which applied to occupiers as well as occupied. Regulations fixed the death penalty for insulting or raping a woman, for looting a shop, or for desecrating a church or school.

My brother Oliver, first born of the family, was old enough to play a small but important part in the bandit game. After six months as negotiator, Father had brought back into law-abiding citizenship all but two of the major gangs. One of the two remaining leaders was named Ding Cu Geng, the other Lu Hing Bang. The latter agreed that he would lay down arms on any conditions the former would accept. Thus one man stood between Father and the stamping out of banditry in the whole Yuki area, peace and security for an area of 2,500 square miles. Chief Ding was suspicious and wily; he demanded a better guarantee even than Father's word. That was where Oliver came into the picture.

Father and Oliver left Nanping for a point sixty miles downstream where General Wang, the military representative, was to be met. They were to go inland for fifteen miles, there to contact the chief. Father felt that if he could actually get word to Chief Ding, he had a card to play that would at least insure a meeting. Accordingly, a messenger was sent two hours in advance of the party to announce to the chief that the "guarantee" he insisted upon would be given.

As usual, there was not a bandit in sight when Father's

party reached the village. However, hanging in a hall-way were two bushel baskets of firecrackers, a half hog ready for cooking, a bundle of pickled ducks, and num-erous freshly prepared vegetables. All the indications were that a high-grade feast was in the offing.

Ere long a slovenly fellow slouched around the corner of the building Father's party was occupying. He stood in the doorway, watching, saying nothing. He looked no different from any one of the score of loafers to be found hanging around where there was excitement, and it goes without saying that there was excitement enough in a mountain village which had just received two foreign devils and a Chinese general on a bandit pacification mission.

Father recognized the symptoms, the cat-and-mouse play that always precedes a meeting with bandits. He was not surprised to learn that the kibitzing loafer was one of the chief's most trusted advisors. He had come to learn exactly who was present, and incidentally to announce that Chief Ding was unwilling to meet with Father be-cause of threatened treachery and the danger of being trapped.

Father was ready. After all other arguments had failed he played his trump card.

"Go back and tell your chief that I have brought with me my heir," Father said, "whom I willingly turn over to him as hostage during our interview. If there is any foul play today my son is in his hands."

The bandit bowed and disappeared.

General Wang and the other Chinese members of Father's party were aghast. To offer one's first born son, one's very heir, as an hostage was unheard of, was almost sacrilege.

Father waited, almost hoping that the chief would turn him down. For it was always possible that a squad of soldiers, traveling from one town to another, might innocently appear on the scene. The military had agreed that all troop movements should stop during days of negotiation, but communications were so poor that orders were not always received; and even if they were received they were not always obeyed.

Suddenly and without warning the chief appeared before the door of the building accompanied by a force of heavily armed men. Both he and his men seemed at their ease while the greetings took place. Oliver was turned over to a squad of ten husky young bandits and told to go and play with them while Father did some "business." Each of his guards was armed with a rifle, one or more pistols, and hand grenades. Oliver had no idea what it was all about, nor did he or my mother know what happened until years later.

Oliver was taken off, and the deliberations started. While the meeting went on, Father occasionally had a glimpse of Oliver and his guards. They were showing him their guns and pistols, and explaining the working of some home-made bomb. The Chief was very proud of those bombs and took pride in demonstrating them to Father. They were made by mixing equal parts of two chemicals, one of which was white, the other bright yellow. The chemicals were purchased, so Father learned, through the agency of Japanese medicine men, at a fabulous price.

Japanese medicine men were a regular phenomenon in the area—and so the role of medicine man had become a favorite disguise of Japanese spies, arms smugglers and opium peddlers.

The bandits had been told that the white powder was silver, the yellow powder gold, and that their combination produced an explosive stronger than anything in the world. To demonstrate the great power of his bombs, the Chief placed a pinch of each powder on the door sill and struck it with a heavy stone-cutter's hammer. The paper on which he laid his fabulous powder was shredded to bits, the hammer blown from his hand. The bombs for which the bandits paid such fabulous prices were used to wreck defenses rather than kill people. An attack upon a barracks was always preceded by the throwing of one or more bombs against the heavily barred doors. The concussion was such as to wrench the whole front off a building and start a panic among the soldiers within. The soldiers seldom offered any defense when an attack was preceded by a bombing.

Chief Ding's bombs having been demonstrated, the party got down to real business. In a few hours Father had succeeded in negotiating a satisfactory deal, one which carried great promise for the abolition of banditry in Upper Fukien. With a considerable feeling of relief,

the party broke up and started howeward in the moonlight. Oliver was enthusiastic about *his* day too:

"Father, those were the nicest men I have ever seen,"
he said. "They even let me play with their guns and one
of them told me that maybe I could spend quite a long
time with them."

Chief Ding came out of the mountains the next day
and spent many days in the command post of the Government troops. There conference after conference was
held to implement the details of the settlement. Everything moved along smoothly, and all concerned had high
hopes for a quick return of peace and quiet to the region.

Suddenly a Japanese appeared on the scene. He ped-
dled medicine among the towns people, and even entered the barracks and the officers' headquarters. No one
to this day knows exactly what happened, but the following morning Ding Cu Geng was gone. Next thing we
knew he was at the head of a strong force of bandits
which he had quickly organized. Never again would he
listen to talk of reconciliation. He had been told something by the traveling doctor which had suddenly
changed him into a raging lion. He wrote Father a long
and appreciative letter, expressing great confidence and
apologizing for his actions. He assured Father, however,
that his actions were justified, as the preservation of life
was recognized as the first law of being.

For more than a year, Chief Ding waged a ruthless
crusade against all his enemies. He even turned against
his former associates who had returned to citizenship,

trying to force them to return to bandit life. He swore to kill former chief Dang Gi Ling unless he would again become a bandit. Finally, he ambushed Dang who was returning to his home one night, killing him and ten others in his party.

Ding Cu Geng's end came in a strange and appropriate manner. With a force of his men he had surrounded one of the stockades, or refuges, that had sprung up all over the disturbed area, and in which soldiers and civilians could seek safety. After subjecting the stockade to heavy bombardment he touched the torch. Every possible exit was covered and any moving object shot on sight. For some reason the chief crept up to examine one of the burning exits. His men did not see him advance, but caught sight of him as he retreated. Following orders, they opened fire, killing him instantly.

I shall always think of the bandits and their sea-faring counterparts as rather brave and romantic men, possessing a sometimes lively conscience. My own only direct contact with these men was with a pirate-bandit-smuggler who played the leading role in Father's last big negotiation which took place not long before he left China.

Years after Oliver's experience with Chief Ding, a communist rebellion broke out on the Lungtien Peninsula. A group of men rebelled against government troops at Gosang, far down the Peninsula, proclaimed an independent, communistic "peoples" government, and prepared to march inland upon Futsing. The leaders of the new Peoples' Independent Republic were one Ung Ding

Buong, and a notorious pirate known as Lo Sie, the Old
Snake, who had graduated from a Christian College in
Foochow and a Church university in Peiping, and con-
sidered himself a "Christian Communist."

The city elders of Futsing at once asked Father and
another Futsing missionary, Pierce Hayes, to mediate.
The usual preparations for "middle-manning" were
made. A messenger was sent to Gosang asking if Father
and Pierce would be acceptable. Ung Ding Buong replied that he would receive the mediators.

Father, Pierce Hayes, and one of the Futsing city elders went. On the outskirts of Gosang, a motley army of
ruffians received them. The first meeting took place in
the Ancestral Hall with the inevitable banquet, this time
a lavish four-table affair. Everyone was friendly except
the Old Snake. When the feast was over the party went
into another room where a conference table had been
set up.

After a few preliminary remarks, Father asked Ung
Ding Buong for his terms. Ung deferred to the Old
Snake who produced a list of demands including everything short of actual abdication of the National Government. But ridiculous and impossible as they were, the
terms had to be discussed politely for a while.

Ung showed an immediate willingness to compromise,
but the Old Snake did not budge. Talk went on and on
through the night, until Father finally abandoned politeness and told the Old Snake that he was talking and acting like a child. On this note the meeting broke up and

the mediators went to bed. It had become obvious that the relations between Ung and the Old Snake were strained. The whole affair began to appear hopeless.

Next morning, the pastor of the local Church of England came to call on Father and Mr. Hayes. He reported that a bitter controversy had broken out between Ung and the Old Snake. The Old Snake wanted to kidnap the missionaries and hold them for ransom. Ung had objected.

The Old Snake was nowhere to be seen during the morning but Ung was about, friendly though obviously nervous. He finally admitted that the Old Snake had left and that, as far as he was concerned, the terms Father had suggested were acceptable.

Father and Pierce hurried home. At Futsing, they found a large contingent of Nationalist Army troops preparing to march on Gosang.

Poor Ung was now left holding the bag. The Old Snake, unable to carry his point on capturing Father and Pierce Hayes had skipped during the night, taking the best guns and troops of the Peoples' Republic. The disarmed Ung Ding Buong had no choice but to surrender, to throw himself upon the mercies of the Government troops.

The Chinese Government had ample grounds for executing Ung. But Father pleaded for his life and Ung was sentenced to a term in a concentration camp where he might repent and reform. He became a model prisoner and was released after serving a short term. Ung Ding Buong returned to his village and embraced a career of smuggling. The Japanese, now engaged in full scale war along the China Coast, hired him as they hired many other pirates. These puppet-pirates, as we called them, manned some of the less important Japanese posts along the coast, assisted in the blockade, and engaged in lucrative smuggling activities.

The United States and Japan were at war, and Ung was on the enemy side. He commanded a large force of armed junks. But he let it be known that he had only the friendliest feelings toward Father. When I came to the Coast as an official of the American Government in 1943, I tried to get in touch with him.

Ung's village was far down the Lungtien Peninsula, and I went forth, ostensibly on a goose hunting trip in his area. The personal loyalty he commanded among his people was immediately apparent. As I approached his village I saw an old woman, working a potato patch.

"Old friend," I addressed her, "can you tell me where I can find the house of Ung Ding Buong?"

The old woman did not even look up from her work.

"Foreign Teacher," she said. "I am but an old woman and I do not know about such things."

I enquired of scores of people, and always received similar answers. I had almost come to the conclusion that he no longer lived in the village, when Ung, who must have followed my search with some amusement, walked up to me. He promised to help me in any way he could; he even said he would try to save American pilots downed in the Formosan channel, if he could do so without the knowledge of the Japanese. He told me in parting that even though he did business with the enemy, he did so reluctantly, and that he hoped some time we would meet under better circumstances.

My life was in Ung's hands on that day. We were technically in Free China, but actually we were in no-man's land. Ung could have spirited me away without trouble. Da Da and I were armed only with double-barreled shotguns. There is no question but that Ung Ding Buong would have been well rewarded by his masters had he been willing to capture an American "spy."

Ung disappeared from our view for a while. The tide had begun to turn against the Axis powers. The Japanese were being pushed back all through the Pacific. Only in China were they still on the offensive, a last ditch offensive as we were to discover later. Ung Ding Buong saw the hand writing on the wall, and the business in which he was engaged must have become more and more distasteful to him.

One day in the spring of 1944, a bedraggled farmer appeared at our home in Futsing and asked to see Teacher Caldwell. He was ushered into Father's study. It was Ung Ding Buong, with a price on his head. He had slipped into Futsing City to ask Father once again to become his middle-man. He was sick and tired of fighting for the enemies of his land. He wanted to surrender his ships and his men. He promised to use his influence to get other pirate chiefs to surrender.

Father immediately told the Nationalist Commander

at Futsing of his talk with Ung. The Chinese General urged him to act as middle-man once again. He told Father that much good could be accomplished by bringing thousands of pirates into the Allied Camp.

But this was an international affair, far beyond other middle-man activities in its implications. Father would be dealing with the enemy, and as a missionary he had no authority to accept enemy surrenders. He urged Ung to go ahead and surrender to the Chinese authorities, but this Ung would not do. Perhaps it was partly fear of loss of face; perhaps also it was distrust. When Father regretfully explained that he could not act in the case, Ung asked that I be approached. Not understanding the vastness of the American Government, he assumed that I as a representative of that Government could accept his surrender.

But I was a mere civilian, two thousand and more miles from my headquarters. Regretfully I sent word to Ung that I could not help.

Ung Ding Buong left Futsing as he had entered, in his farmer disguise. None of us ever saw him again, but once more he was to enter into our affairs. In late 1944, the Japanese made one last gasp offensive along the China Coast. Foochow, Futsing, all the principal cities were occupied. Ung entered Futsing in command of a unit of puppet troops. I do not know how he contrived it, but he managed to get his unit garrisoned in our home and compound.

I do not know how Ung later explained his behavior

to his Japanese superiors; what he did must have been done at considerable personal risk. But he was a pirate with a conscience. Father had acted for him once, had pleaded for his life, and Ung did not forget. While other occupying troops, Japanese and puppet, looted and pillaged up and down the China Coast, Ung Ding Buong zealously guarded our property. No piece of furniture was touched; trunks remained unopened; the garden, the fruit trees, Father's bee hives—all were left just as Ung had found them.

I often wonder about Ung Ding Buong, about all the outlaws of the Fukien Hills and seas, who in the past refused to knuckle under to tyranny. Are the Ungs, the Lings, the Lu Hing Bangs causing their Communist rulers trouble today? Given arms and direction, and above all understanding, will not perhaps these sturdy people provide a deadly obstacle to the solidification of Communist rule? Is there not here an opportunity worth a small investment in time and men?

8

~~~~~~~~~~~~~~~~~~~

THE CITY OF
SOUTHERN PEACE

WE WERE living in Nanping—the City of Southern Peace—in the early 1920's, the years when Father was most deeply involved in his efforts to pacify the bandits. Although we spent five years there, and they were wonderful years, Nanping (in our day it was called Yenping) never quite equaled Futsing in our hearts.

Nanping lies a hundred and twenty miles above Foochow where the Min divides into a giant "Y". Legend has it that the city, built around the prongs of the "Y", was terribly afflicted by floods in by-gone centuries. Each year the two branches of the Min would flood the low parts of town. The wise men were summoned to try what magic spells they could invoke to stop the floods. After fitting meditation, they did arrive at a conclusion. They said the God of the River did not like the way the city was set on the river banks in the shape of the Chinese character for water. If two Pagodas were built, one on each side of the main stream just below the fork, the River God would be happy. So the City Fathers ordered them built, and they stand to this day. But the Pagodas were no sooner than built when a new evil befell the city. It was swept again and again by devastating fires. Now the seers had another answer. The Y of the river, together with the two Pagodas, formed the likeness of the Chinese character meaning fire. Why the Pagodas were not razed to satisfy the newly offended God is not explained. Apparently, the River God had the greater power.

Nanping was a large important Mission station with a number of mission families and several schools. The Foochow dialect was not spoken the country roundabout, but most of the work, indeed the business of the city, was conducted in Foochow, for the Foochow people are the traders and merchants of all Fukien cities, and even, as I have said, of the cities of Malaya, Indonesia, and North Borneo.

Our Methodist compound was high on a hill overlooking the main river. Across a deep valley, the Methodist Hospital could be seen on another hill. Immediately behind the city there is a vast mountain range. Three thousand feet up was the resort of Cha-bang, where we went for the summer. The high mountain behind Cha-bang is the "Top of the World." The whole region is magnificently beautiful and wild. There are vast bamboo and hardwood forests, mountain ranges where even the Chinese have never settled. It is game country of the best but so wild and wooded that the tigers were lost in the wilderness. Around Cha-bang are the silver pheasants, and in the higher mountains, the wild cow of the forest, and everywhere the wild boar, a great beast that weighs as much as five hundred pounds and provided feasts for our table. The pheasants came right to our dooryard and even into it.

The Upper Min is a wild stream, a stream of plunging rapids and swirling whirlpools. The trips up river from Foochow were always an adventure. In those days steam launches could not proceed far above Foochow; and there was not a foot of highway outside that city. When we traveled, we either walked or went by boat. Some-times we would hire for the journey up to Nanping a huge cargo-carrying junk with a long stern-sweep as a rudder, or make it in one or two sampans. It took a full week, for there were miles of water where the boats had to be poled and pulled. A long rope was attached to the bow and a dozen men went ashore and slowly pulled the boat through the white water. And while they pulled or poled, they sang the beautiful wordless melodies of the boat people. At night we would draw aside into some sheltered cove or against a sand bar. We children would be allowed to swim in the clear water and to have a bonfire picnic on the beach. True, there were bandits along many stretches of the river, but we were seldom molested. Our boats always flew the American flag.

It was when we were living in Nanping that Oliver, Morris, and I learned to hunt. I was six then. My first kill was an owl. Father held the gun. I pulled the trigger and was promptly bowled over by the recoil. Young as I was, Father began to take me out after tiger and wild boar. I was with him one day when we saw fresh, oh, *very* fresh tiger tracks. My small legs could not keep up with Father, and I was sure the tiger was at my heels every step of the way. But as time passed, I won my spurs, so to speak. I was standing at Father's side when he shot the largest wild boar he ever killed.

The boar was fully four hundred yards away and looked very small when Father fired.

"Such a small pig," I said. "Where is the big one we were tracking?"

"Just wait a minute," Father answered.

The boar was on a steep slope. He started rolling slowly down the hill toward us. He got larger, his great weight crushing the ferns and azalea in his path. The animal stopped his descent just a few yards from us. Father was right. Eight men were needed to carry the beast to the compound.

In Nanping, also, we first heard the sounds of war, first smelled the stench of death. Roy Chapman Andrews and his wife were with us when the fighting began. Yuan She Kai had just died, and warring factions were fighting for control of the city. The garrison troops had made a deal with bandits to "liberate" the city. Meanwhile an army of Northern soldiers were marching to the attack. The General of the garrison became a bit worried about his alliance with the bandits and treacherously turned on them. Just as this battle was completed, the Northern troops arrived and engaged his forces. For hours, Nanping was in turmoil. Bullets crashed into our house. Father, Mr. Andrews, and Dr. Trimble, our mission doctor, scurried about, trying to make peace among the warring factions. They finally succeeded, and were given credit for saving the city. But to me the most vivid and terrible memory was the stench of the dead bodies that rotted on the surrounding hills for days afterwards.

It was at Nanping that Father received a very strange request. There had been a large-scale battle nearby between troops and bandits. The Government troops were decisively defeated, and many left dead on the field of battle. The Commanding General had lost much face when he lost the battle. But even worse, the bandits refused to allow him to collect and bury his dead. Every time a burial detail went out, it was attacked and routed. In desperation, the General appealed to Father.

"It is humiliating enough to me to have been so decisively defeated," he said, "but if I cannot return the bodies to their own people, I will lose much more face and possibly my commission."

And so Father went out on to the stinking hills with his own burial party, upon whom the bandits did not dare to fire. Each body was placed in a simple coffin, taken into the city and claimed by the family. The distressed commander was satisfied, and the people who lived near the battle ground could breathe once again.

I cannot have been more than eight when I was charged by a leopard. We were pheasant hunting on a hill near the town. I heard Cap, our big pointer, fighting something in a little ravine and dashed to investigate. Cap was tangled with a leopard, but just at that moment he pulled out. I happened to be in the line of the leopard's next move. But Father arrived in time. He dropped the animal at very close range with his shotgun.

It was at Nanping, too, that I earned my first money, nearly seventy dollars. I collected specimens for Roy Chapman Andrews and for Arthur Sowerby, a British scientist. The most celebrated specimen was one that my sister Muriel and I found on a hillside not far from our house. We had gone forth with cyanide jars to collect bugs and beetles. Muriel spotted an interesting snake in the weeds. Snakes are not usually disposed of via the cyanide poison route, but rather are dropped into a pickling and killing solution of formaldehyde. But we did not know this at the time, and after much maneuvering we were able to crowd the furious snake into one of the jars. The snake expired quickly and we went home, expecting praise from Father. The snake was more than interesting. It had a peculiarly shaped head. It had continually struck at us while we were capturing it.

Father took one look at our prize and said, "Where in the world did you get that cobra!"

But the Nanping memories that I cherish most are not

of wars and shooting, wild boars or leopards, but of two men. One was a missionary and an American. The other was a Chinese river boatman who came and went in a single day, and whose name none of us ever knew.

In 1897 a young couple came to China from the State of Washington. James E. Skinner was a medical doctor as was his wife, the former Susan Lawrence. Dr. and Mrs. Skinner lived and worked in many places throughout Fukien, and in each city they left their mark. Dr. Skinner was far more than a doctor. Like Francis Bacon, he had taken all knowledge to be his province. He was a minister, a surgeon, a dentist, and an engineer. A colleague once wrote, "I have been visiting the Skinners and have had my teeth fixed, my shoes resoled, and my eyes examined."

When Doctor Skinner ran out of surgical sutures he made silk from the gut of the camphor moth larvae. When he had nothing else with which to do the job, he made dentures out of bamboo. He built one of the first electric plants in the history of the coast. He planned, with the help of other missionaries, a water system for the city of Nanping, so that today, thirty years later, Nanping is among the few cities of its size in all China to have a water system, crude to be sure, running through leaky bamboo pipes, but still workable.

Dr. Skinner traveled over the central Fukien hills on a balky donkey. He penetrated villages and cities where no white man had ever been seen. His kindliness, his ability to help his fellow man in any situation, opened all doors to him. Almost half a century before the "bold, new concept" of what we today call POINT FOUR was announced, Dr. Skinner brought technical knowledge to the hills of Fukien. Hospitals, power plants, water works still stand as memorials to his selfless service. But the greatest memorial he left is in the hearts of the mountain people. A non-Christian in Nanping once said, "If there is a Jesus Christ and if He comes to earth again, he will look like Dr. Skinner."

Dr. Skinner left the Coast in 1944. It was a final leave-taking. He is now nearly ninety, but even in his old age he is not content to rest. He is operating his own laboratory, making an expensive life-saving serum and selling it at a price that the poor can pay. His two sons are distinguished surgeons. His daughter is missing, lost behind the curtain in Communist China.

The other man was not a great surgeon. I doubt whether he had any education whatever, except what the Min River taught him in a life time of travel with and against her currents. He came into our lives one spring when Mother was away in Shanghai, very ill. Father received a telegram saying that she had to undergo a serious operation, and was hoping he could come to Shanghai at once. A steamer was scheduled to leave Pagoda Anchorage soon, and if Father could make that steamer, he could be in Shanghai within four days.

But the mighty Min was in flood, a flood of such force as few even of the old-timers could remember. Her branches roared into the main river ten and fifteen feet out of bank. The water was rising from moment to moment, and already the lowlands and one city gate were submerged.

Father went to the river to seek transportation down stream. He carried with him a satchel filled with silver dollars. Money was no object; he must get to Pagoda Anchorage. But no boat captain would venture the trip. It was suicide, they said. No boat, large or small, could travel in the raging torrent.

In utter dejection, Father returned to the compound. There seemed no possible way to reach Foochow until the flood subsided, and the fierce downpour still continued. It could well be days before anyone would attempt the Min.

As we sat in sad silence, there was a timid knock on the door. Father opened. A Chinese stood there in the storm, his wet face glistening.

"Are you the American who wishes to go to Foochow?" he asked.

"Yes, I am," Father said.

"Come," said the man. "I have a boat and I will take you. But we must hurry before the waters rise further."

Father snatched his satchel of money and his suitcase and followed the stranger.

The man led Father to a cargo boat tied to a gum tree far above the normal high water mark. In a few minutes preparations were completed, the crew had been given instructions, everything movable lashed down. There had been no time to talk of price.

When a flood is on, the hundred and twenty miles down stream can be run in a day. The boat pushed out into the current and immediately felt the full wrath of the God of the River. For the first seventy-five miles it was swept away on a white-capped muddy torrent. Vast whirlpools tumbled the boat about like a leaf. The helmsman, hanging on the forty foot sweep at the stern, was lifted off his feet and flung about like a snake is flung by a mongoose. At times the boat was completely out of control. At the worst rapids and whirlpools, a crewman was always ready with an offering to the River Gods. He tossed a dish of rice or vegetables overboard, chanting a wild incoherent prayer.

All that day they flew onward and downward, mile after mile, past the mouth of the Yuki tributary, past Shuikow, past Jun-oui-buang. One God or another, the boatman's or Father's, must have been assuaged, for there came the moment when they were catapulted into the relative quiet of the upper tide water above Foochow. The exhausted crew had a respite to eat, to drink tea, and to have a few puffs on the community water pipe.

Now there remained only the few miles to the head of Nantai Island and the Upper Bridge. But the bridge proved another obstacle of a different nature. The river was so high the great structure was almost awash. It was impossible to pass under or over it. The captain ordered the crew to bring the boat alongside the bank of upper Nantai where he hailed a sampan to draw abreast. He quickly had Father's suitcase transferred to the smaller craft, which was light and small enough to thread its way through the flooded olive groves on either side, return to midstream below the bridge, and continue to Foochow.

Being urged to hurry, and with the sampan awaiting him, Father had no time to ask the captain who he was and whence he came. As he was about to step aboard the sampan he opened his satchel of silver dollars to give it all in payment. But the river boat captain refused a single coin. He refused to listen to Father's protests, but turned aside to bargain with the sampan owner over the charge for the next stage of the haul, paying the price from his own pocket. Then, and then only, did he answer Father's appeal.

"Foreign Teacher, there is no charge for what I have done today. You were in trouble, you needed to get down the river. I know few things and have few talents except my knowledge of the river. Those few talents I have are yours to help repay you a little for the things you have done for my people and my country."

"Are you a Church Member?" Father asked in amazement.

"No," said the boatman, "I am just a Chinese boatman and this is my thanks to you and to America."

In these days when we read and hear of nothing but brutality and hatred in China, when missionaries and priests receive not thanks but imprisonment and brainwashing, it is good to remember the simple boatman on the Min who felt he had an obligation to fulfill to *an*

American, an obligation he returned in the way he best knew, and at great risk. It is something to remember.

There is a bond between the boatman's service and the service of men like Dr. Skinner. Dr. Skinner's labor, given in kindness, motivated by love, did not convert all the men and women of the mountains and rivers of Fukien. But love begets love, kindness brings on kindness, bread cast upon the waters is not lost.

9

SUMMER DAYS

ICE AND snow rarely came to our part of the China Coast. Snow sometimes fell on the high peaks about Nanping, on Cha-bang, and on the Top of the World. But the coming of ice was such an event that we children would gather every possible pot and pan, place the utensils out-of-doors at night, and collect enough ice to make ice cream in our home freezer.

Fukien lies in the same latitude as northern Florida. The summer season was always one of humid heat. With the heat came epidemics of plague and cholera and a great increase in the ever prevalent dysentery.

The effect of heat and disease can be told by the tombstones in the cemeteries on Nantai Island. Many of the foreigners, particularly children, died in the summer months.

We had few methods to fight the heat. In Nanping we had no electricity. Power came to Foochow and Futsing but it was weak and fluctuating. In Futsing, our little light plant went into operation at dusk and expired at midnight. Electric fans, refrigerators, other mechanical devices that make summer livable in America were lacking. Our only refrigeration at Futsing was a little screened box called the "hung deu," wind closet, placed outside the kitchen window so that the food would be cooled a little by passing breezes. To get cold, or rather cool drinking water (all of which was boiled first) we sometimes let the water bottles down into the well.

The early missionaries soon discovered the necessity of getting away from the lowlands in summer time. In the late decades of the 19th century, missionaries all along the coast and far inland too, began to establish summer resorts. Summer time meant resort time when we all from up and down the China Coast, picked up, bag and baggage and headed for one of the missionary resorts. There were a number of these in China: famous Peitaho Beach in North China; Kuling, a five-thousand foot mountain mid-way up the Yangtse; Mokanshan, south of Shanghai; Sharp Peak, at the mouth of the Min. We spent our summers in various places, once at lonely Rocking Stone Monastery in the high mountains behind Futsing, a few times at Sharp Peak. I have already told of the lovely resort at Cha-bang, high in the bamboo forests above Nanping.

The resort that all of us remember most is Kuliang.

Kushan, or Drum Mountain, rises 2600 feet from the
plains of the Min. Kuliang (Drum Ridge) sloped down
from Kushan Peak to form a two-thousand foot back-
drop for Foochow.

The beginnings of Kuliang as a summer resort are
shrouded in darkness now. According to the proceedings
of the Anti-Cobweb Society of Foochow—Anti-Cob
was a social and cultural club to which nearly all Americans and British belonged—a port doctor and a Commissioner of Customs first conceived the idea of developing it as a resort. These two together built the first
Kuliang house, but in what year that happened I do not
know.

I do know when the missionaries first began to use the
ridge. It was in the summer of 1887 that Nathan Plumb,
his wife, and their two children camped on Kuliang for
several weeks during the worst heat of the summer. The
Plumb family explored Kushan and Kuliang and discovered a deserted stone cabin, used only for the storage
of crops and tools. Dr. Plumb dickered with the owners
of the cabin and rented it at a ridiculously low price. The
owner was willing to make a deal for the simple reason
that the cabin was haunted. Proof positive was the fact
that everyone who had ever lived in the house had died.

The Plumb family, unafraid of ghosts and realizing
that the one tiny window and door might have had a part
in the demise of former inhabitants, made new windows
and doors and aired and cleaned the cabin. The following summer, that of 1888, "Rest Cottage" was ready

for use, the first missionary home on Kuliang. In the ten years that followed the resort grew rapidly with dozens of stone cottages centering around the Stone Church in which Mother and Father were married. In time, Kuliang became one of the great resorts of China, drawing American and British families from the whole length of the coast.

The move to the mountain was always made in June, the sad move back to the plains in mid-September. After we children were of SAS-age, the summer season was of course determined by the date we returned home from school in the spring and the time we were due back in the fall.

The move from Futsing to Foochow and on across the plains and up the mountain to Kuliang required quite a caravan. From Futsing to Foochow is only forty-odd miles, sixteen overland, the rest by water. Then it is another nine or ten miles to the summit of the mountain. But a fifty mile journey on the China Coast was then and still is quite an undertaking.

The plans for the big trip required much palaver. Da Da had to be dispatched to the Chair Guild to make arrangements for sedan chairs. Arrangements must be made for load bearers to carry the loads. Mother and Chek-Saw, the amah, and perhaps little sister Joyce would ride the sixteen miles over the mountains to Kangcheng. The rest of us would walk. Our loads would require eight or ten coolies, for we took cooking utensils as well as clothes and bedding. The time of departure from

Futsing was settled on the basis of the tide. The Kang-cheng-Foochow launch could pass Kangcheng Creek only with the tide, and go out on the ebb.

Through the centuries the Chinese have developed a simple method of figuring the tides. Take the day of the Chinese calendar, multiply by five and divide by four. This bit of arithmetic provides the exact time that the tide is full at the Bridge of Ten-Thousand Ages in Foo-chow and at Tangtau, on Haitang Island. Through the years boatmen and travelers had figured variations for all the boat landings up the creeks that emptied into the Min. The exact time of high tide could thus be figured for any day of the year, and any travel along the Coast requiring boats was planned accordingly. If the tide were high at Kangcheng at 6 a.m., it meant a very early start indeed. The sixteen mile trip could be covered in five hours. (I set the all-time record myself, walking it in four.) But the chair and load coolies needed much more time. For along the way were tea houses, and at each tea house, one stopped to drink tea or to have a smoke from a long-stemmed water pipe. So the trip required six or seven hours with sociable and sometimes long stops at Jaw-bong, Tiger Mountain Inn, and the other tea houses along the way.

The path we took was an historic one, the flat stones and steps worn smooth by centuries of travel. We passed out of the Little North Gate, up a broad valley, over the fifteen hundred foot Tiger Mountain Pass, finally drop-ping into the tangerine groves along the Kangcheng creek. Then we would fight our way aboard the dirty launch, head down creek for fifteen miles where the creek emptied into the Min River at Pagoda Anchorage and then up the main river to Foochow. The launch schedule was adapted to the tide throughout: down the creek on the ebb, up the river to Foochow on the inward flow.

In Foochow, the rigamarole of hiring coolies and sedan chairs was repeated. The next morning we began the last lap of the trip. The first few miles we travelled by rickshaw over Foochow's one wide street, called the Mah-Dioh or Horse Road. At the end of the Mah-Dioh, coolies and chairs would be waiting for the trip across the plains to the foot of the mountain. Chinese roads crossing mountains are not mere trails. There are thousands of great stone steps, some having served for hundreds of years. The road is always in stages, with a tea house at regular intervals. The five mile trip up the mountain, with tea house rests, always required several hours.

Our Kuliang settlement stretched for several miles along the ridge and its spurs. Many of the older missionary families owned their homes there; they were spoken of as the Lacy House, the Worley House, and so on. Some of the families owned several homes and rented out to those who were less fortunate. Kuliang was laid out in a vast horse shoe with a high ridge in the middle. A path led up the ridge in the middle of the horseshoe, and this path—in steps, of course,—bore the name "Jacob's Ladder." Our social life centered at one end of the horseshoe. Here was Kuliang Village, the Community church where Father and Mother were married; the Club House where we had lectures, plays, and various educational activities. Nearby were the all important tennis courts.

Fukien lies in the typhoon belt of the China Coast and is sometimes hit by as many as eight or nine typhoons in a single season. Most of our Kuliang houses were on exposed ridges, protected by huge retaining walls. For added protection the tiled roofs were covered with rocks. Even so, in a particularly bad typhoon a roof or two would go sailing down the valley. I always enjoyed the "great winds." But five or six days of rain inevitably follow a typhoon, so that tennis was out for the duration. And tennis was the mainstay of Kuliang life.

Kuliang was not particularly beautiful. The hills were for the most part bare, terraced with rice and sweet potato fields. Here and there were groves of bamboos and pines. But there were beautiful spots nearby. Five miles away on the side of Kushan Peak was the magnificent Kushan monastery, set in a grove of trees centuries old. Another path led a few miles to Moon Temple, built into a cliff-side niche almost overhanging Foochow, two-thousand feet below. Eight or ten miles inland was wild and rugged tea plantation country where an aboriginal non-Chinese tribe was settled. There were miles and miles of hiking country, and magnificent views of the vast jumble of mountains inland and the island-flecked sea to the east.

Just as tennis was our chief physical exercise, so the

card game called rook was the chief indoor sport. Rook is often called "missionary bridge" for it is played by rules very similar to those of bridge. But bridge and bridge cards were of course taboo! Rook was an innocent sport that helped while away those interminable hours of rain during and after a typhoon. There were rook tournaments; some persons played as partners summer after summer; some kept the same game going all summer long, until the points totaled in the thousands.

The summer season was not by any means a period of rest only. Missionary meetings, planning sessions were always underway. There were opportunities to compare notes with other workers, to talk about common problems. It was a period of physical and spiritual rejuvenation for many missionaries who spent nine months of the year in lonely stations completely out of touch with the outside world. There was opportunity for Methodists, Baptists, Congregationalists, Church of Englanders, and Presbyterians to get together. Our church services were non-sectarian, each service being conducted by missionaries of different denominations. There were "coffees" in the morning for the missionary ladies; picnic trips to Kushan monastery, moonlight hikes to Moon Temple, sunrise excursions to the top of Kushan Peak. Each year there would be a Methodist picnic, attended by Methodists from all over China; the Congregational or American Board mission would have its picnic. And the biggest picnic event of all was the annual Fourth of July affair.

The center of Kuliang social life, however, were the

tennis courts, and the really big event of the year was the annual tennis tournament. Americans, British, Chinese contended, and there was much rivalry in all classes. Occasionally an American or British warship would touch at Pagoda Anchorage for a few days, and the best Kuliang team would invite the best players aboard the warship to come up for a tennis match. The tennis courts, indeed all activities on Kuliang, were presided over by two brothers named Maiu Kuai and Maiu Kie.

The brothers were sons of the man who rented the first Kuliang house to the Plumb family. They were absolute rulers of Kuliang, controlling the chair guild, the market, and in general making a very good thing of their rule. They decided when the courts were dry enough for use. In return, they were responsible for the scores of houses during the off-season.

Kuliang had one serious drawback for our family, though I suspect that Mother was happy about it. There were no tigers there. Indeed, there was practically no hunting of any kind. Although nearly every summer a leopard would visit the mountain, and we would be notified and spend several afternoons out in a blind with goat and gun, as far as I can remember Father never killed a leopard at Kuliang. But there was much wild and uninhabited country to explore. My Father and I did much of the final research for our bird books while we lived on Kuliang. I spent many hours alone among the cliffs on the side of the mountain. This provided me with an experience that was probably the most important single event in my life, an event that has had a profound effect on everything I have done since.

A little stream sprang from the sides of Drum Mountain, flowing south below the main ridge and the Horseshoe and eventually plunging over a series of high water falls into the Foochow plain. Some early Scottish missionaries had nostalgically named it the Burnie. The Burnie provided us with some big swimming holes, some indifferent fishing—and it made me one of the best known Americans on the China Coast.

There was a concrete swimming pool high on the ridge behind the Horseshoe, but when the boys felt adventuresome we hiked several miles down the valley to the big pools in the Burnie where we could enjoy swimming naked if we wished, where we could be without the "burden" of girls tagging along.

It was the summer of my fifteenth year. Morris and I were considered old enough that year to go up the mountain a couple of days in advance of the family. Other older boys were in our party, our job being to open and air the cottages, to ready the houses for our families.

We had finished our chores. Mother and my sister Joyce were to arrive that day. We boys decided to hike down the Burnie for a swim in the big pool. Three miles below our house there was a fifty foot waterfall plunging into a deep pool, and this was our favorite swimming hole. Below the pool, the Burnie meandered for a few hundred yards and then went into a series of high falls, dropping almost fifteen hundred feet into the plains.

We swam awhile, but during the mid-afternoon tired of swimming, I walked down the stream to the next waterfall. I do not know what I was doing or why I was doing it. I was not, as my SAS school mates claimed for several years afterwards, answering a call of nature. I was enjoying the view of Foochow far below me when suddenly I felt my feet slipping. In a second I was on my way down the falls, bouncing from ledge to ledge. There was a blur of rushing water before I lost consciousness. When I came to, I was far under water in the pool 150 feet below my starting point.

I had been overly modest that afternoon and worn a bathing suit. My first knowledge of injury was when I fought my way to the surface and noticed that my bathing suit, partially torn off, was hanging on one foot. I reached down as I swam dazedly about and tried to pull it up. There was something wrong with my mid-section —I could not bend at all. The pool into which I had fallen was perhaps thirty feet long with sheer walls on all sides. At the lower end there was a flat rock projecting above the water; then a three hundred foot drop down the mountain. That flat rock on the brink of the abyss was the only place I could find to rest, and I swam to it, pulling myself up a bit out of the water so that I could sprawl on the rock.

At first I felt no pain, was unable in fact to realize just what had happened or to understand the predicament I was in. But as the shock of the fall wore off, pain came and I realized that I was badly injured. My face was like pulp. Soon my eyes were swollen shut. One leg was broken and it quickly stiffened. Blood poured from a dozen deep gashes. My forehead was almost split open. A half dozen ribs were broken, or torn loose from their moorings. The most excruciating pain of all came from a little toe which was broken.

I lay on that rock for an hour, calling for help. But the roar of the water drowned out my voice. I have only one clear memory of that stay on the rock. Before my sight failed me completely I saw a green cicada come floating and fluttering by the rock, pause a second on the edge of the great fall a few feet from where I lay, then disappear over the edge. As the insect went over the fall I gave one last shrill scream.

Morris and the other boys finally missed me and came down stream. Morris spotted me from the top of the cliff. He and Bernard Billing found a way to work themselves down to within thirty feet of me. From this point, they dived off into the pool. By now I was so near unconsciousness and so racked with pain and fright that I was in danger of slipping off and following the cicada. By turns the boys held me and comforted me while other boys sped for help.

Meanwhile a new aspect of the drama was unfolding on the road up the mountain. This portion of the Burnie was visible from sections of the road. Crowds of coolies and travelers were watching the rescue efforts. I had been in the pool several hours when help had arrived. My rescuers, accompanied by many Chinese kibitzers, had brought ropes and a ladder and were trying to figure out a method of getting me out of the pool. All this while Mother was riding up the mountain in a sedan chair. As she neared the third rest house she overheard travelers going down the mountain talking about the "Whang-yang"—the little foreign devil who had fallen into the "Devil's" Pool. With each step upward the gossip and excitement increased and she heard the announcement from one traveler that the foreign devil was dead, that his body had just been recovered.

Just as Mother reached a point above the third rest house where she could look down into the valley, my rescuers were getting me out via rope and ladder. A crude litter had been made, and all Mother could see was the crowd of people and a body being carried up the mountain. It was then that she had sufficient courage to ask of the passersby if any of them knew the "Sang," or surname of the boy.

"Why yes," answered a coolie. "One of the Caldwell boys."

Mother could only hurry on to the cottage and there await the final news.

I was not dead—but I was very near death. Willis Barrett, a husky young missionary, had got into the chasm with a ladder. I was placed on the ladder while he swam beside it and pushed it across the pool to the base of the cliff. Men at the top pulled the ladder into an upright position and held it while he climbed, carrying me on his back. The ladder was maneuvered near tiny ledges onto which he would step and hold me while the ladder was pulled up another length. Thus step by step, length by length, I was carried to the top and on up the mountain.

Doctors were called and a telegram sent to Father who was preaching somewhere in the mountains inland from Foochow. I had a broken leg and foot, a viciously fractured skull, broken and cracked ribs, cuts and lacerations, and, still most painful of all, that broken little toe.

As children will, I responded quickly to treatment, and in a few weeks seemed well on the way to recovery. Father and I were planning a big hunting trip later in the summer when I could walk again. I had a pair of crutches and tried them out for short excursions into the yard.

Then the next blow struck. I went to sleep one night full of plans for the big hunting trip Father had promised. A few hours later I awoke with the most frightening headache. The summer season was going full tilt by then, and there were a score of American and British doctors on the mountain. Doctors were called, blood samples taken, a fever of 105 degrees noted. Daylight was breaking when the verdict was announced: Meningitis.

The situation, the doctors told Mother and Father, was nearly hopeless; the death rate from this form of meningitis was very high; the only possible hope, and that a slim one, was to obtain serum for injection into the spinal canal.

Frantic telegrams went out to hospitals all along the China Coast. In the heat of summer the dead must be disposed of quickly, and so my coffin was ordered. Each day special prayer meetings were held for me, each day bulletins went up on the Community Club Bulletin Board. Sister Muriel, graduated from college, was on her way to China to teach, and a telegram, sent to her ship in Japan, told her to expect the worst.

No words can describe the pain of meningitis, the headaches that seem beyond human endurance, the weird phantasies of its delirium. My vision went awry; everything I could see, I saw double. The things I saw that were not there were frightening things. An endless stream of huge rats crossed over the beams above my bed; the nurse became an evil witch, hovering over my bed; great tigers stalked unconcernedly about the room. I can remember seeing Morris and Joyce, peering into the room with frightened faces. I remember Bishop Birney, our kindly Methodist Bishop, coming to pray at my bedside. I can remember, too, of asking for the one impossible thing—ice water. And most miraculous, of having ice water and cracked ice within a day! For there was an ice plant in Foochow, and Father sent Da Da and a special coolie. (The temperature was over one-hundred degrees on the plains that day.) The coolie started out with one hundred pounds of ice. When he reached the top of the mountain there was barely a handful left, but enough to produce a miracle for me.

Just as miraculously, serum came at last. A hospital in Shanghai had the serum, but it could not reach us before ten days. So Da Da was again sent to Foochow to visit every hospital in the city. He found serum in a tiny

The Caldwell home in Futsing, made possible by the gift of a
Tennessee industrialist.

Japanese dispensary. It was an ancient brew, long out-
dated and of Japanese manufacture. But there was no
choice, and so it was used. Then came the afternoon
when a great British brain surgeon came to see me, took
samples of spinal fluid.

He came out of the sick room, test tube in hand. Lift-
ing it against the light for careful examination, he turned
to Mother and Father.

"Well now," he said in his rich Scotch burr, "It looks
pretty good today. I don't believe the laddie will need
any further injection."

The infection had been halted. But by then I was
partially paralyzed.

Moving day came in September, and with it the problem how to move a sick and paralyzed youngster down
thousands of steps to the plain and on to Foochow. A
special reclining chair was rigged up, and I made the
journey carried by six stalwart coolies.

Then came the day when I began to learn all over again
the art of walking. The long struggle seemed to be over.
Bye and bye, I was able to play a little tennis on the court
in our compound. Complete recovery seemed near. But
there was to be no respite yet. A clear fluid, finally identi-
fied by the mission doctors as spinal fluid, began dripping
from my nose. We had no X-rays in those days in Foochow, so that the extent of my broken bones had been a
matter of guess work. It seemed my fractured skull had
not healed, with the result that I was leaking spinal fluid
every day.

The treament was drastic and unpleasant — to bed

again with great sand bags on my head so that I was absolutely immobile. Finally a trip to Shanghai with Mother to see a Russian Specialist who probably did me a great deal of good. He informed Mother in my presence that I had a progressing paralysis on one whole side of my body and would not last very long as a normal boy. When at last I was able to be up and about, I determined to go back to school and lead a normal life. I tried it. Just six month after that day in June when I fell I went back to Shanghai, but I could not yet take it.

The family had by then moved back to Futsing, and there I went. Among the hills of home, along the sea coast, on trips to Haitang Island I slowly found myself again. I shot my first deer that year, saw my first tiger, shot at and missed a big wild boar. With Father or with Da Da or alone I roamed the mountains and got well.

There are more beautiful summer resorts than Kuliang in China, but it is Kuliang that will live longest in the memory of our China Coast family.

10

FORETASTE OF
THINGS TO COME

A LL through my childhood, I heard much about the
menace of Japanese imperialism. The Japanese
were a particularly live evil to our family. During Father's bandit work they had on occasion caused
him much trouble. He was for a long period, unknown
even to Mother, acting as a secret intelligence agent for
the United States Navy, reporting largely of Japanese
activities along the coast.

The Japanese menace was recognized. But there were
few Americans in the early days who talked much of the
Communists. Of all the Fukien missionaries I remember
only Dr. Walter Judd, now an outstanding member of
Congress, speaking intelligently about the Communists.

Yet we all had a foretaste of Communism in Fukien; there was a period when Chinese Communism had its capital almost on our borders. After their break with Chiang Kai Shek, the Communists marched south into western Fukien and Kiangsi provinces and there set up their base of operation, remaining in the wild mountain country until the Long March to the Northwest began. Our first contact with the movement, although few named it such, took place in 1926 and 1927.

We had returned from furlough to the China Coast just before Christmas of 1926. A few weeks before our arrival in China, the armies of Chiang Kai Shek which at that time included Communist units swept through the province on their northward drive. We had missed the main battles, but Foochow and Fukien were far from quiet. Chiang's Revolutionary Army that drove through Fukien was led by Communists and accompanied by Russian political commissars. Michael Borodin, one of the top Communists of the day, was said to be in charge of Fukien operations. He used the now well-known Communist technique of following military victory with vigorous political action. What he accomplished was frightening, for our beloved China suddenly became a most inhospitable place. Day after day great crowds of students paraded in front of the Methodist compound in Foochow shouting anti-American slogans. The phrase "Da-do Meguok"—"Down with America"—echoed all through the day. Occasionally the marchers would stop in front of the compound to spit in contempt. We children

were kept off the streets, watching the parades from behind curtains and half shuttered windows. The American Consul was in constant and anxious communication
with the Embassy in far-away Peking.

What was happening in Foochow was happening all
over the province. The Russian Commissars were fan-
ning a flame of hate, developing an anti-American, anti-
Christian campaign designed to discredit the work of the
missionaries and drive the Americans into the sea. Down
in Futsing, Ling Guang Bing, the principal of our Methodist school, was paraded through the streets, reviled and
beaten. Up river in Nanping, Dr. Skinner was trying to
hold the fort against the Communists who were disrupt-
ing every church service. Ruffians would enter the
churches, drive the pastor from the pulpit, then destroy
every Bible and hymn book in the building. But as fast
as Bibles were destroyed, Dr. Skinner telegraphed Foochow and Father sent up a new shipment.

The Chinese Christians were so terrorized that church
worship went underground. Dr. Skinner himself was
threatened with death. Chinese Christians were beaten
and tortured. By Christmas Eve it appeared that the
Communists had accomplished their announced purpose
of driving Christians out of the city. Nanping was a tense
and frightened city, in the grip of mob rule. But then
came Christmas Eve.

I have described how our Methodist compound there
was on a hill-top; across a valley on another hill was the
hospital; the girls school was on still another hill. Ex-

actly at midnight the strong, clear voices of Christian boys rang out from the Boys' School hill, singing "Silent Night." Like an echo came the higher voices of the girls on another hill in response; then from the Hospital Hill came a bold chant of Christian praise. From all over the city rose the carols of smaller groups. Then hundreds of boys and girls marched down the long steps into the business section. For nine long hours they paraded through that city, singing Christmas carols. As they moved block after block they were joined by other Christians until a vast throng clogged the streets of the city.

The Communists, who had thought the Christian population was completely terrorized, were caught off guard. By the time their commissars had collected their wits, thousands had joined in the carols, fear was gone, further action against the Christians impossible. The carolers then moved to Communist Army headquarters and sang out their challenge. At nine o'clock Christmas morning the exhausted youngsters trudged back up the steps to their schools, so hoarse they could hardly whisper. But they were returning in triumph.

That morning the Political Commissar made an announcement.

"We admit defeat. These people have Christianity in their hearts," he said. "The only way we could stamp it out would be to cut out their hearts."

In Foochow, Communist agitators, still busy with their anti-American propaganda, did not take long to hit upon a device that was a forerunner of the modern charge that Americans are waging germ warfare.

There was a Catholic Orphanage in Foochow. The Catholic sisters often would take the abandoned babies that were found throughout the city and attempt to save them. Often the little babies, nearly always girls, would be picked up so near death that nothing could be done to save their lives. Those who died were lovingly buried in the orphanage grounds.

The Communists conceived a devilish plan. They exhumed the bodies of the dead, took out their eyes, then placed the pitiful remains on exhibit in the main streets. They accused the missionaries of killing Chinese babies, and taking their eyes out to make medicine.

This was a charge that got results among the ignorant. Helped along by professional agitators, a crowd began to attack and loot American property. Several American Board missionaries were stoned and stripped. Then the agitators began to urge the mob on to attack the main prize, the big foreign settlement on Nantai Island, which lies in the Min River and is connected with suburban Foochow by the mile-long Bridge of Ten Thousand Ages. The mob was promised great riches if they would loot and kill nearly three hundred Americans on the Island. Here was an opportunity to drive all the Americans into the sea.

The American Consul called a hasty meeting. He telegraphed frantically for help, and the Embassy answered that an American destroyer was on the way. Since there was always a chance that cooler heads among the Chinese might prevail, the Consul decided to have all preparations made for evacuation but not to leave until the mob started its several mile march through Foochow's southern suburbs and on across the long bridge. Launches and barges were available at a certain jetty; the missionaries who were willing to bear arms were issued guns. The Consul asked Father if he needed any guns, since he already had a powerful tiger rifle. Father replied that he would never use his tiger gun on a human being, and so he was issued a pistol.

Guards and watchmen were mounted at vantage points on the hills overlooking the bridge and the city. It was agreed that the signal for the retreat would be the ringing of the fire bell in a high tower near the British Club. Two men were stationed at the Club with instructions to climb the tower, overpower the guard, and ring the bell when the signal came. Father shared the night watch at the Club with a Catholic priest. Later Father admitted that he prayed hard that the attack would not come while he was on duty. The idea of slugging a fellow human being was most distasteful to him.

The mothers were all busy during these tense hours. Each person was to be allowed one suitcase. So belongings must be sorted and all suitcases must be packed and ready. Thirty minutes to an hour was all the time we would have to get out of our houses, down the long steps to the river, and aboard the escape boats.

A number of men were assigned rear guard duty. Others were to hold the bridge-head, and fight off the mob until the women and children could get safely aboard the boats. It was a time of rumor, of some serious prayer. Early the first morning after trouble had started, a church bell rang to call worshippers to church. Frightened men, women, and children swarmed into the streets, thinking it was the signal bell. No one was following directions. In view of this performance, those in authority decided not to wait for an attack, but to evacuate just as soon as the American gun-boat arrived. It was a wise decision. If the Americans left, perhaps the temptation would be removed and the orgy that seemed in store averted.

The *USS Pillsbury*, number 227 of the U. S. Navy's destroyer fleet, finally moved into the mouth of the Min River under forced draft. Women, children, some of the men moved out, down the steps and on board the escape craft. This time people went in orderly fashion because the attack that had been expected for hours, had still not come. A good many tears flowed as the boats pulled away from the shore because some of the fathers had agreed to stay on. I cannot remember all of the men who stayed, but Father, Mr. Arthur Billings, and Ralph Ward (now Bishop Ward) were among them. The men could take care of themselves if not encumbered by wives and children. They knew the country well, had Chinese friends who would warn them in case of danger, could melt into the hill country where the anti-American influence had not penetrated.

We children did not fully understand the danger at the time. For us it was a glorious adventure. We went down the Min to the Anchorage and crowded aboard the *Pillsbury*. An American destroyer is not made for civilian travel, not fitted out for luxury cruise use. The ship was packed, and until we got well out of the Min River we were not allowed on deck. Every gun was manned; sand bags were stacked about the ship. We sailed down through the twenty-four mile gorge of the Min with every man at battle station. There were Chinese fortifications along almost every mile of the route, on both sides of the river. It was feared that the Chinese would take this opportunity to sink a whole boat load of Americans. When we were finally far out of artillery range, we could shake down for the thousand mile trip ahead—to American territory in the Philippines. We anchored off White Dog Island while the harried commander tried to find room for scores of extra people.

The *Pillsbury* had its crew quarters arranged with bunks in three tiers—triple deckers, not double deckers. There was a scramble for the lower bunks but those who got these places regretted it. That first night was a horror. A destroyer tosses about like a tin can in a whirl pool. Nearly everyone was desperately ill and the occupant of the top or second bunk often did not have time to warn the occupant of a lower berth who was engaged at the same time in the same stomach wrenching activity. By morning the ship was a shambles and the evacuees a miserable lot of people, quite willing to go through Communist torture to escape from their present plight.

As we moved southward the sea calmed. The second

night we older boys were allowed to sleep out on the
steel deck. It was hard, but much preferable to the heat
below decks. We were much intrigued by the flying fish
which plopped on the deck beside us all through the
night.

Whether Americans live in Tennessee or Manila, they
are instinctively kind-hearted, glad to respond to emer-
gencies. At dock-side in Manila, welcoming committees
were waiting for us, and soon we were all billeted around
the city. In a few short days most of us were put aboard
a train and sent northward towards Baguio, the summer
capital high in the mountains of northern Luzon. It was
the off-season in the Phillippines, so there were many
cottages available.

We had sailed out of the Min on the 27th of January,
1927. It was nearly six months before we were able to
return to China. During that period the house in which
we had been living in Foochow was burned to the
ground. We ended up almost stripped of any posses-
sions. All along the Coast and inland other Americans
had the same experience. In some places there was real
violence and American lives were lost. The anti-American campaign slowly subsided and order returned to
most cities. We finally got back to Foochow just in time
for the summer season at Kuliang.

The Communist influence behind what happened then
was not fully understood. Many Americans have forgotten that Chiang Kai Shek tried to work with the
Communists, that he found it impossible, that he saw the

pattern of Communist terror exhibited in China nearly thirty years ago. The lessons of recent history were completely forgotten by American leaders who tried to force Chiang to work once again with his enemies. Few Americans could foresee that even worse persecution and still more bitter hatred, more evacuations lay ahead. For many China Coast families this was only the first of the evacuations that were to come more and more often. For me it was the first of three. The last was in Korea in 1950, nearly twenty-five years later.

〜〜〜〜〜〜〜〜〜〜〜〜

WHAT DO
MISSIONARIES DO?

FATHER always got furious when he encountered the idea, held by so many Americans, that a missionary was a serious, doom-faced gentleman with a Bible under one arm and a black umbrella under the other, interested in nothing but preaching and saving souls. But he was also troubled when he gained more and more fame as tiger hunter, scientist, pacifier of bandits. He began to fear that people might misunderstand the true nature of his activities, the end towards which all his living was directed. Tigers, expeditions into Mongolia, bandits—these were things that provided recreation, true; but far more important, they opened a door into the minds and hearts of people held in the thrall of superstition.

I can remember scores of occasions when the mountain folk came many, many miles into Futsing to beg him to come back with them into the hills to rid them of a marauding tiger or crop-destroying wild boar. But unless the tiger was a man-eater, unless the hunting could further his work, Father would decline the invitations or perhaps dispatch Da Da to do the job. Yet his hunting often did give him an opportunity to advance his real vocation, the preaching of the Gospel. His rifle was a key carried to communities too remote, too anti-foreign to be entered in any other way.

Among the most vivid memories of my boyhood are trips to Baek-leu, a mountain village six miles from Futsing. We often went there to hunt tiger, wild boar, and deer, and always slept in an upstairs room in the house of Deng-po, the village chief. At night, after the hunt was over, after the supper of rice and vegetables and dried fish had been eaten, the mountain folk would troop up the stairs into our room. And then there would be hours of talk, so much of it that my ears and eyes would fail me at last and I would crawl into my cot.

Even people from nearby villages would drop by on these nights, and always the talk would first turn to animals, especially to the tiger and wild boar, and to the perpetual struggle between man and beast. The visitors would ask Father to let them see his rifle; he would explain how it worked, why it was efficient. Soft cries of

"ai-yah" interrupted the intense quiet as he ejected the
cartridges from the chamber and exhibited the smooth
action of the gun. One night a villager brought out his
ancient muzzle loader and every one laughed good-na-
turedly at the contrast between the battered musket and
Father's modern Savage rifle.

As the evening wore on the talk would gradually
veer to other things. The villagers would speak of farm-
ing tools, of how much more efficiently the American
plow works than the simple plowshare of South China
pulled by the water buffalo. Till Father finally eased the
conversation into still another comparison; the white
man's God of love and mercy and the Chinese gods of
fear and cruelty.

"Yes," admitted the head man, "even your God is
better than ours."

Of course, the many who listened to the countless dis-
cussions of this nature that Father started in the lonely
mountain and sea coast villages did not rush forth to
destroy their idols or change their ancient ways of thinking and living. But here and there a seed was planted, a
heart opened, a day school established, an invitation to
preach extended.

Preaching was Father's life, his real work. But the
work of a missionary, whether Methodist, Presbyterian
or Baptist, necessarily includes many other things. The
Methodist Church is a highly centralized organization
with its own bureaucracy and red tape. The missionary
is not free just to go off on his own and remake the

world. The district missionary is appointed by the Bishop to oversee the work of a district in cooperation with the Chinese District Superintendent. In Father's case it was several districts. At Conference time each year, the District Superintendent and Father met with the Bishop to work out the appointments for the new year. Perhaps the preacher in Haikow is a conscientious and able man, but can't get along with his elders. He must be moved. Perhaps the minister at Huang-Dioh is in a rut, psychologically speaking, and needs a change. In the Chinese Church, as in America, there were politics, personality clashes and human frailties.

Behind the Americans and Chinese in the field there was that far-off power in New York, the Board of Foreign Missions. The Board was the final arbiter, paying salaries, settling disputes, planning the work not alone in China but throughout the world. There was one American address we children all knew by heart: 150 Fifth Avenue, New York. It was the address of "The Board," than which there was no greater power save the Lord. One missionary child, studying the Calvert Course, came to his first lesson in American History and Government. His Mother was explaining the exalted position and the responsibilities of the President of the United States.

"Mother," the boy said, "you mean the President is more important than THE BOARD?"

Father was what might be called "general manager" of the church in his districts. That meant not only supervision over the churches and other institutions already operating, but the development of new congregations, widening the spread of Christianity. When he first arrived in China it was often necessary to preach on street corners, to spend hours and days in talks with a man whom one had a slight hope of converting. Later, when the church was well established, street corner sermons were discontinued. Instead, Father would conduct prolonged evangelistic meetings, in district after district, village after village, assisted by the Chinese preachers.

During the many months I was home recovering from my accident and illness, I often accompanied Father on his evangelistic tours. Da Da usually went along, and we had two load coolies to carry the cots and bedding, and the small amount of food we took. For the most part we ate Chinese style and slept in the churches. Now and then a family would put us up.

Father was, and still is, a fiery preacher, whether in Chinese or English. He was so vigorous, so prone to waving his arms and shouting, that I was often embarrassed. But his style was extremely effective. The Chinese loved it. At the close of each service those who wished to embrace Christianity were asked to come forward. Often the converts would bring their household gods and ancestral tablets with them, and when the suppliants had been accepted there would be a great bonfire of gods and goddesses of every description. Converts could not immediately be full-fledged members of the Church. They must enroll in classes, must go through a period of study, before they could fully satisfy the Church that they understood the Scriptures and the full significance of the action they were about to take.

Much of Father's energetic work was attempting to divert the superstitions and traditions that sapped the spiritual and economic resources of the people. The economic toll of superstition is tremendous, with innumerable gods and devils to be placated, and the priests drawing fat rewards for doing the placating. Father has been known to put his reputation and the power of his God squarely on the line in his fight to wean men's minds from irrational beliefs.

There was a hill not far from our home which was said to be a "spirit hill." The wildcats and foxes living on it were "spirit cats," capable of taking wing at night to fly down and kill the poultry on the nearby farms. According to local lore, no man had ever been able to waylay a spirit cat and bring it in alive or dead. Father told the people that if he, or Da Da, could not kill one of the animals, he would agree that his gun, even his religion, was inferior to their "spirit religion." Accompanied by a great crowd of hunters and sightseers, Father headed for spirit hill. On the way he saw a wildcat, shot at it and missed. Fortunately, spirit hill was a long way to go and the people paid no attention to that miss. But Father realized that next time he must shoot to kill. He got the first "spirit cat" flushed out of the sword grass on the hill. A few minutes later Da Da made a second kill. That ended the nonsense about *one* hill in China.

Early missionaries were particularly shocked by the Chinese way of disposing of unwanted babies. It was done in a number of ways. Sometimes the new-born were simply abandoned; sometimes there were special pools for drowning them. In Foochow there was a "baby disposal tower"—like an incinerator. Near one mountain village there was a sacred grove of pines with a huge camphor tree at its center. At the base of the camphor tree were dens of wildcats, and the tiny victims were stuffed into the dens alive, or left just outside. Naturally the whole grove was over-populated with well-fed foxes, wildcats, and wolves of a so-called "spirit" variety. Indeed, in this particular spot throwing away babies had almost acquired the characteristics of human sacrifice. One could gain special grace and dispensation by sacrificing one's baby to the spirit animals.

Father built a church near the grove. Within two years the ancient camphor tree was cut down and the custom completely and permanently ended.

There was once a baby drowning pool in the outskirts of Foochow where one could count from half-a-dozen to a dozen bodies any day of the week. With a special gift of forty dollars Father built a school in the vicinity. I remember that pool vividly because one day when I was small I caught my first specimen of the beautiful Memnon swallow-tail butterfly as it hovered over the flowers blooming in what had once been a place of death. I read the Chinese words on a little stone tablet, at the edge of the basin:

The drowning of Children in this Pool is Forbidden.
Although babies are still abandoned in China, the missionaries have come very close to stamping out the barbarous custom. I know of no "drowning pools " anywhere in Fukien today.

In his sermons, Father would lash out at customs of this nature, speaking with inspired vehemence. At other times he would build a church or school nearby, hoping that the influence of Christianity would be strong enough to make people see the evils of their beliefs.

It can be argued that there were many converts who still had little knowledge of what they had professed; it has been argued that they professed Christianity in order to get better jobs. Such converts were called "rice Christians," and doubtless deserved the title in many cases. But there were thousands for whom conversion meant a totally new life, a life free of devils and demons, free of the myriad ancient superstitions that bound their minds as well as their feet. It meant an opportunity for children, especially for girls, to get an education. It meant a new viewpoint on matters of public health—and above all it meant a new awareness of the importance and dignity of the individual, of his obligations to society. There were few practicing Buddhists in China, few but the long robed scholars who knew anything of the wisdom of Confucious' teaching. Christianity filled a great gap, made for a fuller life, for men and women more able to play their part in the unfolding drama of China's rise towards real nationhood.

Father preached scores of times each year, planning out his services in Chinese rather than English. In fact on his long trips into the country he thought in Chinese. (It is a curious fact that one dreams bilingually: often in childhood, and still now occasionally I dream in the Foochow dialect.)

After his retirement, Grandfather Caldwell came out to China for a visit. He had a long white beard in the old southern tradition. His age and his beard made him a subject of much veneration among the Chinese and a successful evangelist among the heathen. He would preach while Father or Uncle Ernest would interpret. This combination was very impressive, and the father and son teams were much in demand all over the four coastal districts. Grandfather was especially interested in opium and directed many of his sermons against this evil.

He was an old man when he came to the China Coast, but he adapted himself well except in the matter of some of the outlandish dishes of the Chinese. Father and Uncle Ernest revelled in trying to get him to eat certain things he had declared he would never touch. He was especially vehement in his condemnation of snails, jelly fish, young octopus, sharks' fins, and such like delicacies of the sea. On one occasion Dr. Li Bi Cu, chief of our Futsing Hospital, gave a big feast in his honor. There were many dishes of the sea and Grandfather carefully inspected each course before eating. One innocuous-looking course he liked very much and asked for several helpings of what he thought was a noodle of some kind, cooked in a delicious sauce. After the feast was over, he inquired about the dish. To his horror he discovered he had eaten three helpings of "swa-chengs," the juicy angle-like worms that live in the sand all along the Fukien coast.

Grandfather came for a visit. He stayed for two years of active missionary work. It was a fitting climax to his years of service as a minister, missionary to the Indians, circuit rider, and educator.

Because a vigorous Christian enterprise must include buildings, churches, schools, parsonages, and hospitals, the district missionary has the task of developing a building program. During his years in China Father was responsible for 108 buildings, and in some cases he literally did the building himself. Cement and concrete were unknown in Futsing when he came. His building of the first concrete wall in Futsing was a real event. The elders and sages heard that the foreign devil claimed he could build a pillar that would stand upright without support. By the score they kibitzed as he directed the making of a wooden form, and himself poured the concrete into it. When sufficient time had been allowed for the concrete to dry, it was announced that the form would be removed, that Teacher Caldwell guaranteed the pillar then would be firm, would stand of its own strength. There was much comment among the people with the sages maintaining that the pillar would fall as soon as the wooden forms were removed. A gasp went up from the crowd, some of the less brave souls jumped back to be out of the way of the falling pillar. But it stood there, strong and firm. And thus came about a little by-product of a missionary's work.

Father not only built the churches and hospitals: he also supplied the water needed for the buildings. For Father has that strange and disputed talent of being able to locate underground water with a forked peach stick. He is, in the language of New England, a "Water Dowser." His abilities along this line created quite as much comment and argument in China as attends the exploits of water dowsers in America. There were among his missionary colleagues some who would never believe in his forked stick, who made much fun of his "water witching." But I have seen him find water on many occasions. His standing agreement with well diggers was that if water was not found where his stick indicated an underground stream, he would pay double the standard price for digging. He never had to pay up.

His batting average was so perfect that he was called upon for water witching as often as for tiger hunting. Sometimes he was called in after a half dozen dry wells had been dug. Once the Methodists planned a big new hospital at Lungtien City. The only available property was purchased, but before construction began, well diggers were called in to find a permanent water supply. Five deep holes were dug, and all were dry. The whole project bogged down, plans were made to build the hospital in another city, less desirable and twenty miles distant from the people it was to serve. Father heard of the trouble, went to Lungtien and found water within a few

feet of one of the dry wells. Father found wells throughout his four coast districts, for churches far up the Min
River, at Bishop Gowdy's home in Foochow, and for
summer homes on Kuliang.

The cost of building 108 Christian edifices, the cost of
equipment, the money needed for all the many facets of
a great missionary enterprise did not grow on trees. Chinese Christians slowly moved towards self-support, but
much of the money for the enterprise had to come from
America. Money raising required much of Father's time,
time he felt could be ill spared from more pressing matters. But this was a part of the work, a very necessary
part.

Each morning after prayers Father would devote several hours to the task of writing Church people in America for help. Literally thousands of personal letters went
out from Futsing each year, to travel across the ocean
into American homes. Before the days of the mimeograph
this was a formidable task. Many of the gifts were small,
some ranged as high as $25,000. Many donations were
for general work, while others were for specific purposes. Thus it was that John A. Patton, Chattanooga industrialist, gave money specifically for the building of
our home in Futsing. W. P. Copeland of Clark Mills,
New York, "built" the main church and our home in
Nanping. John B. Meyers of New Orleans provided the
funds for the lovely church in Futsing. Dr. John
Goucher, well known Baltimore educator, provided
funds for the building of twenty churches along the

coast. Mrs. Luella F. Stewart of Wellington, Kansas, gave the money for the fine church at Sungchung, near the headwaters of the Min River. Dr. Merle Smith of Pasadena, California, made the main church building on Haitang Island a memorial to his father. A woman in Florida had willed her estate to a dog and cat hospital. She was prevailed upon to shift her interest, with the result that her gift of thousands, together with more thousands from a church in Des Moines, made possible the building of a magnificent boys school in Futsing. Men and women, rich and poor, from all over America played their part in the work that was carried on in Fukien.

Many missionaries are supported by a church in America, are carried as regular members of the church staff. For most of their missionary years Mother and Father were supported by the First Methodist Church of Wellington, Kansas.

The church people in Wellington were kindly folk, and would have smiled at the nervous apprehension with which we visited them on furloughs. Mother would carefully drill us on how to act and what to say. I almost spoiled church relationships when we visited there during Halloween. The Halloween customs of American children were strange and fascinating. It was not with too much difficulty that the Wellington boys persuaded Morris and me to join in their fun. They explained that one old custom included ringing doorbells, then running away. I was elected to ring the doorbell of an imposing residence. I did not realize that one of my mentors was just behind me with a bucket of water. When the door opened, my friend tossed his water and disappeared. I was too stunned to move. The gentleman at the door turned out to be the Sunday School Superintendent of our supporting church.

The Wellington people were kind indeed, loyal supporters of a life's work. During the early 1930's, when Chiang Kai Shek's government began enormous public works programs, and roads were built in Fukien Province, the church collected money to provide Father with a car. For months the Sunday School children of Wellington rolled their pennies, nickels, and dimes up to the altar in toy cars. And before long sufficient money was available, and a brand new Plymouth on its way.

Now Father could reach many of the churches by car. Futsing and Haikow were connected by road with the little town of Huang-dioh, six miles west and inland. Huang-dioh was on the new coastal highway linking Foochow and Amoy and touching many of the church towns in Father's districts. The Wellington car also stream-lined tiger hunting. Father and Da Da could jump in the car and be within a mile of a tiger lair within half an hour. The Wellington Church Plymouth is probably the only car to come into its home garage with a tiger draped over the hood!

Chiang's roads and the Wellington Car made work easier, placed Futsing a little nearer to the rest of the world. It soon became possible to drive to Foochow in three hours. The long trip from Futsing, over Tiger

Mountain Pass to Kangcheng, the long hours on a smelly river launch became things of the past. Hardy travelers even began to drive overland clear to Shanghai, or south to Amoy. But there were still scores of mountain villages into which Father must walk, there was still Haitang and Gong-ing Island accessible only by junk. And there were still bandits in the hills and along the new highways.

The strain of constant travel, preaching, letter writing, conferences, and planning tired missionaries quickly. In spite of summer months spent at Kuliang or other resorts, life was hard on Americans. Disease, physical or mental, took its toll. Every five to seven years, differing with various denominations or according to climate, the missionary had home furlough, a period of recuperation.

Furlough was a great but not unmixed blessing. Preparations for the steamer trip up the coast to Shanghai, then the long trip across the Pacific, started weeks in advance. And life in America after one or two months of travel was not entirely easy. The Mission Boards were hard task masters even though the year at home was supposedly a time for rest. There was always more money to be raised, speakers from far away China were always in demand among the churches, there seemed to be almost as many planning and policy meetings to attend as in the U. S. Department of State. Father rarely had any rest, and often was away from home for weeks on end on extended speaking tours. His responsibilities were no greater than those of all "vacationing" missionaries I have ever known, as a child or at the present time. Whether one be Baptist, Methodist, Congregationalist, or Presbyterian, home leave is a time for speech-making.

And for us children, furlough was often pure hell. Our clothes brought from China were home made or ordered long ago from a mail-order catalogue and hardly in style. In China we had had no opportunity to learn games that American children have known from infancy. But above all we lacked the knowledge of how to get along with vast numbers of at times very cruel American children.

I remember particularly the furlough we spent in Seattle when I was ten years old. For the first time in our lives, Morris and I attended a public school. We tried to play baseball with the other boys, but having never played before we were awkward and threw like girls. Our clothes were different. We picked up new words without meaning to us, repeated them at home and were punished or reprimanded. The harmless taunt, "Chinky Chinky Chinaman," was hurled at us when our background became known, and we ran home crying. Then, just when we had become used to life in America, just when we had nearly forgotten our native Chinese, just when we had at last made friends, we were uprooted and off we went back to China.

For Mother and Father, furlough did mean many good things. They visited relatives and childhood friends, and we were all able to savor long forgotten luxuries—running hot water and flush-toilets were those that most impressed me. While we might enjoy luxuries, we certainly did not live in luxury. The missionary's salary that went far enough to hire several servants in China was barely enough to live on in America. There were few extras that we could afford.

We were very poor, but I do not remember that we looked like tramps when we were on furlough trips to America. In Seattle, Morris and I had just two white shirts, but those shirts were washed and ironed each night. The young Caldwell boys might not have been dressed in style, but we were dressed clean. The style among young boys that year was to wear sailor suits. At a cost of $9 each—and that was a fortune in our family—Mother had bought sailor suits for Morris and for me. With the ingratitude of youth, we refused to wear the new outfits, preferring to keep our ancient and out of style Chicago mail order suits. A vivid memory I have of these years in the homeland is that of going into a hotel in San Francisco, and of the treatment we received. We were due to board ship for China in a few days. When Father tried to register his brood, he was rudely turned away. Suddenly it seemed there were no rooms available. Morris and I were old enough to realize that it was not a problem of space but of appearance. And we had no idea why our appearance was such that we were not allowed in a second class hotel.

Thus did a missionary work and live. While Father would say that the preachings and the conversions he made were of the greatest importance, I think it difficult to separate from the sum total of his—and other missionaries'—work the vast number of projects carried on to make life a bit more comfortable for the people of China, a bit more civilized. The missionary's contribution to a fuller life has been complete. There were of course "bad" missionaries, men and women who by their narrowness of vision or for other reasons were simply not adapted to a productive life on the China Coast. There were those who fell by the wayside, there were those who could never master the languages, those who stayed on in spite of unfitness. But most of the men and women of my childhood were men of Dr. Skinner's ilk, men of extraordinarily broad interests, who brought to China not only a religion of love but the very foundations of democratic progress.

There was little denominationalism among the missionaries of the China Coast, and I regret that I write more of Methodists than of others. Actually it was only during the summer months that we saw much of our Presbyterian, Baptist, Congregational, and Church of England colleagues. The task was so vast, the field so broad, that the churches early adopted a policy of dividing up the country so that there would be overlapping only in the large cities. In Fukien, the Church of England worked the territory north of the Min River mouth. In Foochow, several denominations were active. Then Chang-lo County, just north of Futsing, was Congregational territory. Father's four coastal districts, Hing-wha and Sienyu to the south were Methodist; then came a large Church of England area, and finally in the southern part of the province there was a large and active Dutch Reformed Mission.

This same pattern was followed throughout China. The Baptist missionaries were active in Kwangtung province, south of our borders, the Presbyterians in parts of Central China and the Far North, the China Inland Mission in many sections of the interior. Here and there were independent missions, such as the Christian Herald Orphanage in Foochow. Sponsored by the Christian Herald Magazine, this institution became a model in the training and education of orphaned and under-privileged children. Its shops produced outstanding craftsmen, its class rooms outstanding Christian leaders.

Father was not actually an unusual missionary, except perhaps for the part that tigers and hunting played in his work. There were other missionaries who hunted, who killed tigers even, who played a large part in the scientific and cultural development of Asia. Their impact on the Far East has never been fully appreciated by Americans.

From the time when William Carey, perhaps the first Protestant missionary, arrived in India from England in 1794, the missionaries have had a tremendous effect upon the development of the Far East. Carey entered his life of service with a verse from Isaiah 54 as his charge: "Enlarge the place of thy tent—lengthen thy cords and strengthen thy stakes." He followed this injunction; it played a tremendous part in broadening his years of service.

Carey was among the first men to advocate forestry practice in India. His protests began the death knell of infanticide in India. He translated the Indian classics into

English, so that the West might learn a little of the East's culture. Carey had his problems, among them the misunderstanding and suspicion accorded to his work by the diplomats of his time. He was forced to begin his ministry in the city of Serampore, then under Danish rule. The East India Company, diplomatic representative of the British Crown, was convinced that missionary work would arouse resentment among the Indians, would jeopardize the Company's rule, order, and profits.

As I have said, men like Dr. Skinner of Nanping began Point Four work many years ago. Even long before his time, there were men like Timothy Richards, a Baptist missionary in North China, who worked for flood control, public health, and better transportation. Years before the Wright brothers invented their plane, Richards predicted that aviation would one day solve China's transportation problems. As early as 1885, he advocated the exchange of students between China and the West as a method of producing international understanding and peace.

The life led by missionaries improved, of course, with time. The days passed away quickly when, as in Judson Collins' time, missionaries were stoned. But life was never easy, there were heart-breaking disappointments. So often the Lord seemed to throw great obstacles in the way of his servants.

But the day Father got his automobile seemed to be a day of promise for China Coast missionaries. China was awakening, physically and spiritually. Chiang Kai Shek's

Father's 60th birthday celebration. The city fathers gather to pay homage.

new roads were but a surface indication of the new China, a land that now welcomed missionaries. Had not the ruler of the nation himself embraced Christianity? But even as a new day was dawning, new trouble was in the making. A period of war and bitter struggle was just over the horizon.

The Japanese began with an attack on Shanghai in 1932. After a few years of uneasy peace they struck again in 1937. I was the only member of the family not in China when the long war began. Oliver and Morris now were educational missionaries, teaching at the University of Nanking. Muriel and John Pilley were teaching at the Anglo-Chinese college in Foochow. Joyce was spending a post-high-school graduation year at home in Futsing. The Japanese invasion changed the course of all our lives, as it did for other China Coast families. Morris hurried back to America to enlist in the air force, to be trained for the struggle he felt was inevitable. Oliver played a large role in the heroic evacuation of a great university, starting with the Rape of Nanking and ending far in the mountains of China's west. Muriel and John soon took part in an evacuation too, following their school into the mountains. But it was upon Mother that the greatest blow fell, it was she who suffered most.

12

~~~~~~~~~~~~~~~~~~~

FUTSING DIARY

AMERICAN housewives might be inclined to envy a missionary's wife. Mother had no cooking to do, an amah to look after the babies, someone to do the washing, the marketing, a boy to wait on table. Of course, there were children to teach during most of the years in China. But teaching took only half the day, and even with it Mother's life would not appear weighed down with burdens of undue hardship.

Yet, actually Mother's life was an extremely rugged one, lived without most modern conveniences, a life requiring fortitude and faith, a life full of worries and tragedies. There was the death of Gail, the third child, of dysentery in the days when a ready cure had not been developed. There were hours of sleepless fear when Father and Da Da were tiger hunting or conferring with bandits, and returned late or not at all that night. There was arduous missionary work to be done, and much travel over the country with Father.

I think that Mother was often afraid. I know that she worried much. But she had a tremendous dedication to her task as wife and mother and missionary. It is difficult now to remember her in the early days when she was able to walk the mountain paths with us, before her copper-washed hair began to turn to grey and white. Her life was truly one of a pioneer wife. In addition to the years in China, we spent two years in Alaska. We saw no news-papers, indeed lived so far from the nearest settlement that we visited it twice a month. Whether it be in Alaska, on a destroyer evacuating the family, at home in Futsing, Mother was, I believe, the real strength behind Father, behind us all.

Mother had a difficult language to master, strange etiquette to learn, customs to observe which must have seemed outlandish to a girl from Tennessee. But more trying by far than all this were the horrors of the Japanese conquest of Fukien.

After years of debate, the Methodist Church in America had united its southern and northern branches in one large denomination. The Uniting Conference of the church in China was scheduled to meet in Shanghai in early 1941. This was an historic occasion, finally joining together the work begun in Foochow in 1847 by the northern church, with that established in Shanghai by the southern branch of Methodism a year later. Father and Pierce Hayes, also stationed in Futsing, were elected delegates from the Foochow Conference to the uniting meetings. In normal days, the trip to Shanghai and back would have been fairly uneventful. But these were not normal days.

The Japanese had occupied North China and were beginning a blockade of the China Coast. It was a period of tension, but missionaries who have gone through war and civil strife stick to their plans if it is humanly possible. Father and Pierce calmly set about running the blockade. They started for Shanghai perfectly aware of the situation, but not believing that the Japanese would make any landings during their absence.

Mother stayed on in Futsing for two reasons. She wanted to be near my sister Muriel and her family (they were in Foochow, forty miles away), and she keenly felt the responsibility of a missionary's wife to give aid and hospitality to foreign travelers and refugees at such a time. Haikow, the port of Futsing, had become a busy and more or less clandestine sanctuary for the little coastal steamers. The screen of outlying islands made it an ideal spot for breaking the Japanese blockade, and so Futsing had become a point where missionaries and foreigners congregated as they slipped in and out of the province. Even as Father and Pierce were about to leave, a German family, trying to return to Germany before hostilities spread, had come to our house to await transportation. Mother felt she could not leave her "guests." Indeed, our home had become a hostel in a city where there were no hotels.

Father and Pierce reached Shanghai safely and attended the conference. But in their absence the unpredicted happened. The Japanese made a landing along the coast, preceded by wide-scale bombings. In a few months Foochow was cut off from Futsing by the Japanese and by bandits. The blockade was tightened, and Father was stranded in Shanghai for weeks. He finally caught a British ship to Amoy and walked the hundred and fifty miles north to Futsing. Meanwhile, let my Mother's diary tell of her months alone in Futsing:

"*March 8, 1941*. . . . Poor Tangtau on Haitang Island was terribly bombed last week. We don't know how many of the people were killed but Ding Do Huak, a retired local preacher was simply blown to bits. No trace of his body had been found. I suppose some Jap airman is proud of his marksmanship—I simply don't know what to do about the people who come in here when the air raid warning is given. They are no safer here I am afraid than they are outside and they fill our shelter so we have no place to go. Perhaps the downstairs here is as safe as any place, as long as the bombs are small.

"*April 19th*. . . . Yesterday there was a siren and we heard the planes but couldn't see them. This morning at 5:30 the alarm woke me up. This is the first time we have had one so early. The children couldn't go to school. We saw the planes. Twelve seemed to go northwest. (Afternoon, April 19th) The planes have been over all day. We have had many "urgent's" but none came near until about 3:40. Then a plane came over, circled several times and dropped two bombs somewhere near the Little North Gate, or where it used to be. Sing Kie says the soldiers are fighting pirates near Diong Loh and that the Japanese are helping the pirates. My ears seem to hear that old warning bell all the time. My heart sure does a lot of hard work when the planes are around. . . . I hope they did not bomb Foochow today, I wish Muriel wasn't so afraid of them. My heart beats fast but I have no great fear. If I am hit I hope I won't be an invalid.

"*Sunday, April 20th*. . . . It is now just 4:15 and I am downstairs. All night I heard excitement and confusion but slept quite a bit in spite of it. Once when I got up I could see the lights carried by people moving across the fields west of the house. Mr. Ding called me to give me the rumors. He says the Japanese have landed at Sung-a and he thought we should leave. But where can we go? Bandits probably at Derng Diong, no launches on the River. I am praying God will guide us and help us do the right thing. If Harry and Pierce were here I would have no fear. 11 a.m. A plane has gone over several times and used its machine guns. Chek-so and the baby also Ai Cio and others have gone out about a mile from the city. They took some food and bedding and there will await developments. . . . Poor Muriel (in Foochow) will be so worried if we are occupied. There has never been so much air activity before. It must mean something. Evening, April 20th. I'm afraid I'll never forget this day. I was glad to see the sun go down. Planes over all day.

They machine-gunned. I got tired of the shelter and finally stayed in the house. We now have Da Da, Bo Muoi, Sing Kie, his wife and four children, Bo Muoi's old aunt—all to spend the night with us.

"*April 21.* . . . There was a big fire at the North Gate and when we woke up a little after three there was a huge fire near the South Gate. There were soldiers all night in the house near us. Evening. All day we expected the soldiers or the tu pi's (bandits) to come knocking on our gate. We could hear them all over the city breaking into houses. About four the servants, Sing Kie's family, and our other guests saw a soldier carrying a Japanese flag paste something on our gate. Sing Kie and I went out to see. Just as we went out we saw a bunch of soldiers turn the corner. I felt like running but decided we had better face them. We saluted and they saluted. They were very orderly. I was thankful to have the first meeting over. The paper on the gate says, "This is foreign property. No one is to enter here." I felt weak with relief. Last night the parsonage was looted.

"*April 23.* . . . A very quiet night. We have just had prayers. I hope that they comfort these who are with us as much as they comfort me. We know now that Foochow has been occupied without a fight. I wonder how Muriel is taking it. . . . Ding Sing Ek's slave girl was in their house yesterday when "they" broke into it. They broke into everything. She climbed back under the eaves and hid there until they had gone. . . . A company of cavalry just passed behind the house. I wish I could get in touch with some responsible officer. I would feel so much easier.

"*April 24.* . . . Last night I dared undress and have a bath. . . . I have an idea we Americans will have to leave soon. I wonder when and how. My how I long to see an American *man*.

"*April 25, 5:10 a.m.* . . . A battle is raging around us. I had hoped we would be spared this but it has come. I was awakened about three by the sound of cannon. . . . then the rifles and machine guns began. It was all around us for about half an hour and then moved toward the West Gate. I hope and pray that God will make it possible for us to get away. I hope we can plan for all these with us here.

"*April 26.* . . . The guns kept going until about 11:30. It was quiet all afternoon until about four when the big cannon behind the house fired. . . . All morning no one dared venture into the yard. It was such a blessed relief when the big gun stopped firing. It shakes the whole house when it goes off. I do wish some responsible person in the (new) government would come to see us. Da Da seemed to think the Chinese would try to recapture the city last night. So I had Sing Kie's family sleep in Pierce's room and old I-muoi and Bo-Muoi's sister-in-law move in from the Gate House and sleep in the study. We closed all the shutters tight and tried not to have a glimmer of light showing. I didn't want our windows to be a target for any one. . . . A while ago I heard fire crackers and rushed up the back steps to look out the window. We saw a strange procession. Practically all the merchants from the street were bearing gifts to the conquerors—several big fat hogs and jars of wine. Well, I don't blame them at all. They must settle down to something like living. They can't spend their days hiding in the villages. I do hope the market opens up so the poor people can buy and sell.

"*April 27.* . . . Late yesterday the messenger came from Foochow with letters. He had them rolled up in the hem of his trousers (to escape the Japanese guards) and they were so wet we could hardly read. Muriel's letter was very short. She says they are packing but gives no inkling of their plans. Last night I could not sleep for worrying about getting the messenger off to Foochow. I was afraid if they found our letters on him they would shoot him and arrest us. We sent three tiny letters wrapped in oil paper. Once more they were sewed in the hem of his trousers. Then I gave him twenty Chinese dollars. This he carried in the top of his hat. When he passed a sentry he takes off his hat by grabbing the crown.

"*Monday, April 28th.* . . . After breakfast we had prayers. Mrs. Uong, Ping Ga's mother is here. Things are very bad down country. While I was resting after prayers I was called to the gate. Three Japanese were there, one rather a high officer. They said the American consul in Foochow wanted to know if we were all safe.

The message came by radio. They were most polite and kind and I wrote out a message for them to send to Foochow. Then I sent them to Edith's, after serving tea and cookies. (Edith Abel, who lived across the city in the Girls' School Compound). I hope they comforted her as much as they comforted me. I may try to send a message to Harry in Shanghai. God is good to us.

"*April 30th.* . . . The end of another sad day. . . . This morning I went over to Edith's. The planes were flying around when I got there. Shortly after arriving I heard bombing. Not long after I got back I heard that Baek Bu Muoi was bombed and Mrs. Hung Kuang was killed. Later Edith came to tell the whole sad story. Gung Chuang's daughter is dead, his son is wounded. King Hung the carpenter is dead. His wife is wounded.

"*May the First, 1941.* . . . Alas another sad day. Da Da has left for Foochow. Lying awake last night I felt that was the wisest thing to do. If he gets through safely he can guide Dr. Skinner down. I shall pray continually for God to walk with him. Sad stories come to us. I cannot bear to write them down. I think if Dr. Skinner comes he can persuade the commander in charge to put a stop to the killing.

"*May 2.* . . . I heard shots out Derng Diong way. The battle lasted about two hours. Mrs. Li came to get medicine for poor Mrs. Hung. She carried it out hidden in the bottom of a little basket of fruit. It was anti-tetanus. . . . The battle in the hills is over now. I wonder how many innocent people were killed. The stone mason's family stays here all the time now. She is a young mother with two small children. Another young girl came in this morning, running away from a soldier. We now have seven women and five children hiding in the compound. Dear Lord, care for them. They, the children—are playing happily in the yard.

"*May 5th.* . . . Today Da Da got back and tomorrow I am to try to go to Foochow. Chair men and Load men are coming for me tomorrow morning. I'll spend tomorrow night in Da Da's home village in the mountains then on to Dai Ngie Wednesday. Dr. Skinner and Martha (McCutcheon) will be there to come back here in our chairs. John (Muriel's husband) will meet me and return to Foochow with me. Am I running away from my duty? I pray not. Harry is still in Shanghai. I wonder if he and Pierce will ever get back here?

"*May 9th.* . . . Many things have happened since I wrote. We had left Loung Tau (Da Da's village) about five-thirty and were in Dai Ngie at 7:30. There we waited two hours for Dr. Skinner and Martha to come in the launch. They came at last but in a small boat. Martha had seven thousand Chinese dollars with her but had arrived safely thus far. We said goodbye very quickly. I got in the boat with my refugees and we started for Pagoda Anchorage.* But alas, in fifteen minutes we met

* NOTE: The usual route to Foochow via Kangcheng and Pagoda Anchorage was closed by the fighting. Mother and Da Da traveled inland to the south branch of the Min River, then down river to the Anchorage.

bandits! And I spent one of the worst fifteen minutes of my life while they threatened to take John and I Daik if we didn't give them ten thousand dollars. It finally ended with their taking everything I had plus John's raincoat and ring. Poor Harry's two fine cameras were part of the loot. If I had not been so frightened for fear they would take John I might have saved some things. . . . Well they finally let us go. The next two hours were terrible as we expected to be held up again any minute. But we made the Anchorage at last. It was after seven when we got here (Foochow). Poor Muriel was frantic of course.

"*May 17th.* . . . Foochow. Yesterday we heard many explosions. They say the Japanese were blowing up houses at the West Gate so the Chinese won't have them to hide behind. . . . I feel very badly now about having left Futsing. Da Da was supposed to go back to Dai Ngie to try and contact the bandits to find our things. He went a week ago. I think I'll try to send another messenger in a few days.

"*May 19 (Foochow).* . . . Last night I stayed up to listen to the Mail Bag from Treasure Island.* I heard from John. It was sent to "Mrs. H. R. Caldwell, some-where in the Orient." I suppose the children think we may have been evacuated. Da Da came yesterday after-noon. He wants me to get some sort of official paper from

* NOTE: By mid-1941, mail service to much of the China Coast became impossible. Radio Station KGEI in San Francisco accepted messages to be broadcast in the hope that missionaries here and there would pick them up. This was my only method of communication with my parents in that year.

the Consul authorizing the bandits to give me the things; or he wants John or me to go and get them. . . . in a little while I am going to see the Consul.

"*May 23 (Foochow).* . . . Yesterday Da Da got back again with two loads. The cameras are safe. Many things are stained and messy, but most of the clothes can be salvaged. Da Da paid out $256 "ransom" to get the things back. . . . Many small boats went up the Min yesterday carrying Japanese soldiers. I wonder how many of the poor fellows will return. The Chinese guerillas seem to be giving the Japanese something to think about. There are many tales of truck loads of dead going through the streets.

"*June 5 (Foochow).* . . . A telegram from Shanghai. Harry has finally left for home via Amoy. I hope and pray Harry gets a boat up here, but I am afraid there isn't much hope. I wish I were in Futsing. How sorry I am that I came away.

"*June 7 (Futsing).* . . . Here I am back in Futsing. I hated to take the trip back. I was full of a hundred and one fears. Although the messenger and others were sure I could get through safely, I was still afraid of the bandits. No foreigner has traveled the old road since the invasion so I wasn't sure just how the bandits would treat a "Whang Yang" (foreign devil). I don't think I would have been brave enough to take the trip alone but Uniola Adams wanted to come down to try and help out, so I felt I had no excuse for not coming. Thank God for giving me the courage to come. I feel a little less ashamed for going away in the first place. It was a little after two when we got to Kangcheng and there was a sedan chair and two load men waiting for me. . . . They finally decided we should stay there all night and get an early start in the morning. This we did and were off about 6 a.m. We met our first bunch of bandits near Changtao about six miles from Kangcheng. They didn't stop my chair at all but Uniola was walking, and she says they asked for five dollars. . . . We met the next bunch on top of the big mountain, and the messenger says when they saw our name on one of the baskets the head man said: "Don't touch those baskets. They belong to Mr. Caldwell." So we passed the last danger point.

"*June 28th.* . . . About two o'clock on Friday the Hing Wha messenger came to tell us that Harry and Pierce were waiting about five li (two miles) outside the city to learn how to proceed about getting in. Sing Kie took a relative who speaks Japanese and went to meet them. There were five of them with six loads. It was one a.m. before Pierce and Harry got here. They had been on the way one month, and it is nearly four months since they left here. I am so glad this hard separation is over. And how glad I am that I was here to greet Harry. Now the Bishop and various people are suggesting that Harry go home alone for his eye operation (cataracts) and I stay out here with Muriel and John. I am not at all sure if this is the right thing to do.

"*July 13th.* . . . There have been a number of cannon shots near the South Gate this afternoon. There is quite a little talk about the guerillas attacking the city, but there was no firing during the night.

"*July 20th*. . . . Just three months since the "occupation," and today there must be more Japanese in the city than Chinese. Since eight-thirty we have watched them pouring into the city over the Huang Dioh Road. I wonder where they will quarter such an army. Yesterday afternoon they brought in some stretchers, and later we saw the smoke of a huge fire when they burned their dead. It makes one fear for the women and girls to have such a huge army in this little place.

"*July 20th*. . . . This is little Robin's second birthday. (Robin was Muriel's first child. Gail was to be born in November, in Foochow where Muriel and John were still expecting momentarily to receive orders to evacuate.) How we wish we were in Foochow. And oh if I only knew what we ought to do. Now no one is allowed to come in or go out except those living within one po (three miles) of the city.

"*July 29th*. . . . Yesterday ten girls and six boys came over from Haitang. They want to go to Free China to attend school. Last night the boys slept on the study floor. The question is how to get them out of the city . . . with relations so strained between the U. S. and Japan our position is anything but pleasant.

"*August 3rd*. . . . I have been back here a little more than a month. I realize now that Harry and I should have left much sooner. Now there is no telling if we can get out at all. Harry feels his eyes are failing fast and is of course much worried over the prospect of being shut up here for some time. We must face the idea of a concentration camp. And it just depends upon how severe the restrictions are as to how many of us survive the ordeal. Relations between the U. S. and Japan are rapidly nearing a crisis. The time may come when I may have to destroy this journal. If we don't get away this week we may not get away at all.

"*August 4th.* . . . This morning Harry sent Sing Kie and Tung Tung to interview the commander about permission to start south for Amoy. It was refused. So we are stuck probably for the duration. If we are to be in a concentration camp, I wish we could be with Muriel and John and Robin. We hear that in Foochow there are sentries at all the compound gates but we don't know if this is just a rumor or the truth.

"*August 7.* . . . Yesterday Pierce had a letter from Zela Worley with quite a bit of Foochow news. There are sentries at the gates, and they will not allow anything to go out or in. What is Muriel doing about fresh vegetables? The consul is trying to get a boat in for those who wish to leave. Harry and I are asking the consul to help us get to Foochow. There is a proclamation on the street that the people are not to sell us anything without the permission of the Mi-ti-huoi (local Government under the Japanese). Before the fifteenth we have to tell them how much money we have in the bank and all about any property we possess. . . . I think we have enough stores in the house to last us three or four months . . . if we can only get a few fresh vegetables until the garden begins to bear. I hope and pray Harry and I can go with Muriel.

"*August 24th*. . . . Harry and I are still here and have no hope of leaving. It has been a quiet week until last night when there was quite a bit of shooting. The "occupiers" are supposed to be retreating. For days stuff has been moved out of the city. There has been a letter from Bishop (Carleton) Lacy explaining his advice for us to go to Minchiang. He thought we would like to move up river with Muriel. I would gladly move up there; I guess the best thing for us to do is go to the USA. Sometimes I get terribly homesick.

"*August 25*. . . . Last night the big guns behind the house fired towards the west and northwest. . . . Every shell must have dropped in a different place. If only "they" would leave. We hear that the Chinese in the Japanese Puppet Government are shedding many tears. They know that when the Chinese come back they will probably be executed. I feel sorry for them. Many of them were forced into doing what they have done, into being traitors.

"*August 26th*. . . . We were awakened by cannon fire about an hour ago. The Japanese have been withdrawing for several days. Yesterday the weather changed and we seemed to have a little typhoon. To the South of the city there is quite a flood. We wonder how the attackers expect to get into the city. The Japanese seem to expect them though, and the boom of the cannons behind the house shakes the house and makes the windows rattle. . . .

Harry, Pierce, and Dr. Skinner are listening to the six-thirty news from Manila. There is a lull in the fighting so they can hear. . . . The Japanese sing song girls or the "rose buds" as we call them left about noon. Harry and Pierce saw launches simply jammed with people. All the Chinese the Japanese have been training here went with them. Also families of the Puppet officials. Poor things. They are now considered traitors to their country and simply have no place to go. We hear that Foochow is being evacuated, also. We do pray that those who come in will not be worse than those who leave.

"*August 27th*. . . . All day we have been running in and out of the shelter. The planes have dropped dozens of bombs in the villages all around us. There are still Japanese in the city. How I wish they would all get out tonight. There may be terrible disorder when they leave, but what a relief it will be. We were able to buy a bag of flour today. We paid $110 (Chinese) for it.

"*August 28th*. . . . Evidently there are still a number of Japanese here. Yesterday when they fought out at Guang Ing Buoh there must have been quite a few Japanese killed. They began yesterday afternoon to burn bodies, and there have been big fires all night and all morning. It is cloudy today but no rain or wind. I wish there would be a storm so these awful planes would have to leave. "Brownie" (the dog) is getting thinner and thinner. Many days she won't eat at all. The big guns behind the house nearly drive her crazy. If this keeps up it would be a mercy to kill her.

"*September 1, 1941....*"The Second World War" is two years old today. And what a dreadful mess this whole world is in. This morning about nine o'clock Japanese soldiers surrounded the house. Nearly a dozen had crowded into the gate, and before I was able to get down stairs they were on the verandah. The Su-Beng (Commanding Officer) sat down. Everyone else stood. They wanted to search the house and every man, woman, and child was to be brought before them.... It seemed that one of their Chinese soldiers deserted after extorting large sums of money from other Chinese. Now they are trying to find his wife and six day old baby. Someone told them the child was born in our compound. Well they finally seemed to believe us.... The bombing today has been terrible. I feel as if I couldn't stand many more days of this, but I suppose I can if I have to.

"*September 2nd....* Once more we are living in Free China! Last night just before dark the Japanese shelled the little villages just to the west of us until I felt like crying. Things were quiet when we went to bed at eight-thirty. When the guns began booming again a little after three Harry who had been sleeping on the verandah came into the bed room. We didn't get up until we realized that shells from the big guns were falling just outside the wall. Harry, Pierce, and I got dressed and came downstairs. The Skinners stayed in bed as the shells were not bursting on their side of the house. Pierce went into the attic to "see what he could see." He was sure he could see Japanese soldiers in the orchard outside our wall, on the hill behind the house, but just a little later he saw a lot of Chinese soldiers in the orchard just outside the wall. They wore straw hats covered with leaves. A plane came sailing in from the sea. The Chinese soldiers immediately disappeared under the trees. Before we ate breakfast Pierce and Harry saw puppet troops leaving the city by the south gate and (Chinese) troops leaving the city by the west gate. Before daylight we heard a lot of excitement. I think the Japanese must have retreated just about that time.

"*September 3*.... A lovely cool morning and the very air seems different now that THEY are gone. Yesterday was a great day for this little town. If it hadn't been for the death-threatening planes I think the people would have gone crazy with joy. All morning we were running in and out of the shelter. But finally with the American flag spread on the lawn we just stayed in the house downstairs. After the planes left the new magistrate returned to the city. He had been hiding out in the hills all day. And how the people welcomed him. I never heard so many fire crackers in my life. About five-thirty the district superintendent and the pastor came in with one of the old city fathers to invite the men folks over to a meeting and a victory feast. It seems a shame to waste so much money on a feast, but we can hardly blame the people for trying to express their relief. Many women these four months have hardly dared to leave their homes. Last night they were all out and so happy they did not know what to do. Thank God THEY are gone. Now our only fear is the planes."

And so, after bombs and battles, peace came to Futsing, the Little City of Happiness. But it was a peace of short duration, and it was not the true peace Mother had prayed for. Twelve years have now gone by and that peace seems farther off than ever.

THE BEGINNING
OF THE END

THREE months after the last entry in Mother's
diary, the Japanese struck at Pearl Harbor. Life
as it had been on the China Coast was a thing of
the past.

The Japanese blockade became water-tight. Ships
could no longer slip into Haikow or Santuo. The Japanese launched a massive drive southward across the heart
of China, and soon the whole coast was cut off from the
rest of the world save for a narrow corridor. The China
Coast from Shanghai south to Canton and for hundreds
of miles inland, became a vast no-man's land, nominally
under Chinese control but always subject to enemy forays. The outlines of no-man's land were vague and chang-

ing, depending upon the temper of the people, upon seasons and crops. What was today a bit of Free China might tomorrow live under the flag of the Rising Sun.

Now more than ever, the bombers came, ceaselessly, by day and by night. The enemy was always just beyond the horizon, and his agents were everywhere. When his bombers came over, they knew what and how hard to hit.

People changed their habits to meet the working schedules of the bombers. Multitudes, driven from home, drifted from town to town in search of hope and refuge. Colleges and universities "refugeed" far into the interior. Missionary families moved too, or stayed on with escape route planned, essentials packed, farewells spoken, ready to move when the enemy landed. The names on the map might speak of Happiness but the mood of the Coast was of terror and heartache.

Muriel and John, their son and new baby, fled far inland, up the head-waters of the Min, to the little river town of Iongkau. There the Anglo-Chinese College began a refugee existence that was to last for four years. Schools, government offices, business establishments, all moved so that soon the center of Fukien existence had left Foochow, and gone far into the mountains of the upper Min.

For Mother and Father, too, Pearl Harbor meant many things. For months, letters to China had gone the long way around, across the Atlantic, across Africa and India, then over the "Hump" into China. Many letters became casualties of the voyage. Until Pearl Harbor Day there had been one method of communication that occasionally got through. San Francisco's radio Station KGEI on Treasure Island broadcast each week a "Mail Bag" program. Messages were read out over the air, in the hope that Americans in lonely mission stations along the coast might pick them up. Thousands of anxious ears strained toward San Francisco and the impersonal voice of a faraway announcer who might bring words and news of loved ones. But this was a one-way street; word could go out to China, but no answer was possible.

Thus it was that we in America did not know what was happening on the Coast. After Pearl Harbor, KGEI discontinued its "Mail Bag" for security reasons. The long route through the back door of China was still open, but now many letters fell victim to enemy submarines that infested the Atlantic, to enemy planes that preyed among the mountain passes of the Hump.

We at home could not communicate with the Coast, could not know of things that befell our loved ones there, could not tell them of the things that befell us. And the war soon began to change our lives.

Morris was the first to go. He had volunteered for the Air Force and had received his commission as a fighter pilot a few weeks before Pearl Harbor. Two days thereafter he volunteered to go on an expedition to relieve one of the hard beset garrisons of the Philippines. His unit crossed the Pacific by ship to Australia, crossed the great deserts to Darwin in the North, island-hopped to Java.

By the time they had reached that island, relief for the Philippines was out of the question. American forces were fighting a rear guard struggle on Bataan and Corregidor. Japanese troops were swarming into the Far South, were landing on Java itself.

In spite of the Japanese victories, of the threat of their complete triumph in Asia, the radio telephone service across the Pacific was still intact and operating on March 1st, 1942. On that day Morris called me in Nashville from his air field in far off Java. He wanted news of Father and Mother, wanted to warn me not to worry if I did not hear from him for a long time. He knew, but could not tell me, that Java and all the East Indies were lost, that he and his unit would begin to withdraw the next day in hopes of reaching Australia or India. But the next day was his last day. He was killed, his plane shot down in flames, as he and his comrades were attacking a Japanese cruiser.

All this I tried to tell Father and Mother, by letter, by cable, by friends who were going eastward and might meet them or get news to them. I wanted also to tell them that I was volunteering and would try to work my way to the East.

By now, escape to America was impossible for Father and Mother. The sea lanes were closed. Allied planes that flew the Hump into India were so hard pressed that no civilians could be taken. Father's health, already poor, became worse. The news of Morris' death finally came through to them. Worry, the loss of Morris, difficult living conditions conspired to make Father's eyes deteriorate rapidly. The cataracts that had been forming for months now almost blinded him. It was decided that he must have an operation at once but there was no doctor in all of No-Man's land who could perform that operation. He would have to reach West China, would have to cross No-Man's land, through the corridor into Free China and on to the Far West where hospital and medical facilities were available. It was a trip of 3,000 miles that faced two tired old people, a trip that must be made by every imaginable conveyance, with enemy planes and enemy troops never far distant. Pierce Hayes went along for company and for help.

The first leg was easy and over the well beloved path to Kangcheng. This old route of travel by sedan chair and launch had to be taken once again, for the highway over which Father and Mother had been able to drive their car had been destroyed by the Chinese Army in efforts to make all Japanese advances slow and difficult. From Foochow, they traveled up the Min to Nanping by river launch. From Nanping the route led for nearly a thousand miles south and west, across the high ranges of the Bohias, by bus to Kukong on the headwaters of the river which flows into the sea near Canton. At Kukong they transferred to the section of railroad still operated by the Chinese, and traveling by night to elude enemy bombers, they reached the American airbase at Kweilin

in China's southwest. From Kweilin onward to Chungking and Chengtu travel was simple, in airplanes fur-
nished by General Claire Chennault's "Tigers." In this
way Father reached a Mission hospital in Chengtu, almost
in the foothills of the Himalayas.

The cataract operation was successful and Father
could soon see once more, though his eyes would never
again be quick and alert enough for tiger hunting. It was
still not feasible to fly out of China; Mother was loath,
too, to leave Muriel and her children. So they retraced
their steps—and by plane, rail, bus, river launch, and
sedan chair they took the long road back to Futsing. Over
five thousand miles had been covered before they
reached home again, and twice they had crossed the heart
of a great nation at war.

Oliver and I, meanwhile, had been exerting every
effort to get into the Armed Services, hopeful that we
would end up in China. We volunteered our services to
every branch. Because of the waterfall accident I could
not get into Army, Navy, or Air Force. At last I was able
to get an assignment with the United States Office of
War Information. Soon after Father and Mother had
completed their trip to the West of China, I was on my
way across the Atlantic by freighter, on across Africa,
the Middle East, and India by plane—bound first for
Chungking and eventually for the China Coast. For I was
to become an American Information Officer in Fukien,
the land of my birth which I had not seen for twelve

years. Oliver too was soon in uniform, a Captain in the Office of Strategic Services, bound for duty in India, Burma, and West China.

It was September, 1943 before I reached the Coast. For nearly three months I stayed in Chungking, China's war-time capital, doing nothing while my superiors talked endlessly of policy and plans. I was shocked at this my first taste in the operation of foreign affairs. I was shocked because I was getting the largest salary of my life, plus an enormous living allowance—and was doing nothing. I was shocked because there were many others similarly employed while a war was going on.

At last I was able to shake loose the shackles of red tape and headed south and east, to Kunming and Kweilin by air, then over the same route Father and Mother had traveled on into Fukien. Along the route I got my first taste of modern warfare, crouched in dug-outs and trenches while Japanese planes strafed and bombed, saw for the first time the wreckage of once prosperous cities and villages. And I became intimately acquainted with the wondrous air raid warning system of China, a system which knew the exact moment when Japanese planes left the run ways at Canton's White Cloud Air Field, or the fields of the Yangtse valley and then by siren, by bells, by "callers" perched on high platforms, foretold the exact route, progress and destination of the planes. I experienced for the first time the tremendous spectacle of a whole city of 100,000 souls emptying into the surrounding hills when the enemy approached.

It was thrilling to come home to the land of my childhood, strange to be coming through the back door, across the heart of China into Fukien from the West. On the afternoon of the fifth day on the bus, inappropriately called the Kukong-Nanping Express, I saw the first land marks of my childhood—the towering cliffs of the Top of the World, next to it Mount Discovery, and Mount Washington. Then to the north of where I knew Nanping lay, I could see the unbelievably rugged Pass of Three Thousand Eight Hundred Steps, which led across the mountains to Iongkau, the refuge of Muriel and her family. Nearly twenty years had passed since I left Nanping as a small child.

From a hill top I got my first view of the city, the City of Southern Peace, and of the compound where we had spent five years, from whence Father had journeyed on his trips among the bandits. Below was the huge Y formed by the converging branches of the Min. I saw the two Pagodas and recalled the ancient story of their building and the disasters that came to the city.

As the dusty bus rolled into Nanping's bus station at the foot of the Methodist Mission Hill, a small miracle occurred. As I stepped off the bus, Muriel was walking down the street. My coming was unknown to her. She had just that morning come down the river from Iongkau to visit a refugee dentist.

I stayed in Nanping just long enough to rest, to see old friends again, for I still had one hundred and fifty miles of travel ahead of me before reaching the coast. I stayed with Fred Bankhardt, father of my childhood classmate of two decades earlier; I visited with other missionary friends of by-gone years. Then I started down river on the last lap of the journey to Futsing, for it was there and all along the coast that I hoped to do my work.

There had been many changes in river travel since my childhood. The sampans, the cargo boats, the ugly craft known as the "A-mo Ka's"—The Old Duck Legged Boats—were still on the River. But instead of going down stream in one of these craft, I traveled on the *S. S. Fukien,* a river launch operated by the Min River Steam Navigation Company. The down river trip by launch took just one day, the up river trip a day and a night.

From Foochow on to Futsing travel was as I remembered it—down the river to Pagoda Anchorage, now a dead port, fifteen miles or so up the creek to Kangcheng, where load bearers and a chair awaited me, then the sixteen miles across hills and mountain passes to Futsing.

In my childhood days I had always looked forward to the point on the road where the great towers on the city wall above the Little North Gate first came into view. As I approached the city now I saw no towers, no city walls, no gates. The three-hundred-year-old protection against bandits and pirates had been torn down; for the Chinese had discovered that the high walls provided the same protection to victorious Japanese occupiers as they did to the original inhabitants. The enemy could take a city, hole up inside the city walls, and make day time forays into the surrounding country side. As the fine highways of Chiang Kai Shek had been destroyed, so had the great walls of the Middle Ages—all in defense against a new enemy.

The sun was dropping behind the Derng Diong Pagoda when I entered Futsing. A cool wind came in from the sea. Just inside what had once been the Little North Gate a small crowd had gathered. There were Da Da, Pierce Hayes, and Father.

Father was emaciated and for the first time in my memory, he looked old. Things were the same, yet different. The same huge banyan tree still stood behind the house, the tree in which we children once had a tree house among the sprawling limbs, where a black-eared kite always nested in the highest branches. But now the tree house was gone. Instead, there was an air raid shelter at the base of the tree and extending under its giant roots. And just as I entered our compound I heard a sound not known in my childhood—the air raid warning bell among the banyan trees in the old Yamen began to ring. I was to hear its tolling, and that of bells like it, a hundred times in the year ahead, and my way of living was to become attuned to the manner of the ringing. Pealed out slowly, the warning meant that the "bamboo telegraph" reported Japanese planes leaving runways somewhere, on some airfield. Rung more quickly, it told us that the planes were heading in our direction, were not far off. A frantic pealing of the bell indicated the enemy were over the Province, in sight of the nearest warning posts.

The planners in Washington had told me that my job

was to inform and educate, and in that process to give hope to the war-ravaged Coast. I was to talk of America's military might, of the certainty of Allied Victory, of great air fleets in the building, of the promises to mankind in the Four Freedoms and the Atlantic Charter. I was to talk to the people and their leaders, to set up exhibits, to fill the newspapers with stories of America's might and America's good intentions.

As I tried to carry out my instructions, I found that the work of Grandfather, of Father, of Muriel and John before me opened the people's ears and hearts to my message. No one ever doubted the truth of what I said. Though a foreigner, I could stand without fear before large and excitable crowds. In fact, the only thing that ever scared me about my work was a reprimand from my superiors in far-away Chungking, who started to get jittery when they realized that every word I was saying could not be checked and double-checked. But very conveniently I became ill when they tried to recall me, and by the time I had recovered they had received sufficiently good reports about the effects of my work and decided to leave me alone.

During my year on the China Coast, with headquarters in Nanping, I worked and traveled throughout the length and breadth of the Land of Happiness. Sing Kie, of Mother's diary, was my helper, and my interpreter where the Foochow dialect failed. Together we walked almost the whole coastline of the province, for the highways had all been destroyed. In between trips, I had occasion to visit briefly in Futsing. I hunted ducks and geese in the memory-haunted mud flats near Haikow, visited again the mountain village of Baek-leu, and slept again in Deng-Po's upstairs room. On the outskirts of Baek-leu there is an ancient pine tree, a tree which had borne, eleven feet above the ground, the claw marks of a tiger at which Morris and I had ogled on boyhood hunting trips. A new set of claw marks had taken the place of the old, looking no different to me than those of fifteen years earlier.

Deng-Po had heard the news of Morris' death, and asked about the circumstances. Morris' story was an impressive one, for in China the sons of the influential did not go to war, and we were influential people on the Coast. It was much commented upon that in democratic America even the son of a great tiger hunter fought for his country.

As the tide began to turn against the Japanese, the situation along the coast became more tense. It was feared the Japanese would make one last drive into all parts of Free China, would make one last-gasp offensive. There was more activity along the coast, Japanese armies in the Yangtse Valley began to show signs of restlessness. On May 15th, 1944, I received a confidential letter from an American friend in Kweilin. He wrote:

"There is no official sanction for this letter or even any knowledge on the part of higher authorities that I am writing it. . . . Without going into detail I should just like to say that if I were you I would be west of the Hankow-

Canton railroad at the very earliest date possible. I would not delay much past May 31st. You may like those hills of Fukien but I wouldn't like to see you wandering about them with nothing much but a tooth brush. I would advise withdrawing all equipment with you. . . . I cannot too strongly urge you to accept this advice and act upon it immediately."

This was chilling.

A few days later the remaining American missionaries along the coast received a communication from the American Consulate in Kweilin. Marked "Strictly Confidential" and couched in State Department prose, this communication gave a similar warning to the missionaries:

"Acting upon the authority of standing instructions from the Department of State, this Consulate strongly advises that all missionaries who can possibly do so withdraw from southeast China to places of safety to the west of the Hsiangtan-Hengyang-Kweilin railway system. Those persons who remain in the vicinity of this line of communications or to the east thereof render themselves liable, if not to capture, at least to complete isolation for the duration of present hostilities. . . . Arrangements have been made with the United States Armed Forces for the transportation by air from Kweilin to Kunming of American citizens returning to the United States, especially women and children and invalids."

The memorandum ended:

"The Department has directed this Consulate to emphasize that it has been found extremely difficult to arrange repatriation of American citizens captured by the Japanese during military operations."

I could well imagine what might happen to men like myself if we were captured. The prospect of capture, of long isolation, was not a happy one for me, but it was inconceivable for Mother and Father. They already had gone through enough trials and heartache. In a few weeks the warnings were heeded. As the only civilian official on the coast, I was to arrange for the evacuation to the west. I myself, with a promise from one of my superiors that if worst came to worst I would be picked up by a fighter plane, and with a strong feeling that my job was still unfinished, decided to stay on for the time being.

As the Air Force would provide transportation from our great air base at Kweilin, my problem was to get the missionaries to Kweilin, or even better, to one of the closer advance fields in Kiangsi Province. We managed to make arrangements with the 14th Air Force to pick up the refugees at one of these bases, some three to four hundred miles to the west.

Word went out to all the remaining active mission stations, to Futsing and Hingwha and Sienyu on the coast, to the stations on the upper branches of the Min. The word was to meet in Nanping as soon as possible for evacuation.

I had made good friends with the Provincial Governor and through him I arranged for the chartering of buses and trucks. The missionaries began to converge on Nanping shortly after the first of June, and on June 18th, 1944, Father and Mother left Fukien, never to return. With them went Muriel, John and the children, Dr. and Mrs. Skinner and many others, Methodist, Congregationalist, and Church of England. There was no denominationalism in that evacuation. Just before the caravan pulled out, two Catholic priests arrived in the city on bicycles. They were stationed one hundred miles to the north and, hearing rumors of a Japanese advance, had gone out on their bikes to investigate. There was an advance, sure enough. It was so fast that the Fathers were cut off from their home and came on to Nanping with what they had on their backs. There they joined the other evacuating missionaries.

It was a sad occasion. Da Da came up from Futsing with the family. Church leaders came to say goodbye, probably also to envy those fortunate ones who had the means of escape. There were many tears along with many fire crackers. Father told me of their leave-taking in Futsing. Father and Mother had walked through the house for one last look at the things that had made up our home for so long. They said good-bye to the servants, all but Da Da. There was much sorrow.

Then, with the few pounds of baggage allowed them, they started on the road to Kangcheng. It was raining, but a huge procession followed them out of the compound, through the remains of the Little North Gate. The Chinese offered presents, but they could not be accepted. There were many in that throng who were not

professing Christians. There were city and county officials, generals and privates, reformed and unrepentant
pirates and bandits, teachers, smugglers, fishermen, men
and women from the hill top villages. Many of them followed all the way to Tiger Mountain Pass, a few even on
to Kangcheng and Foochow.

It was in Foochow that Father finally agreed to accept
a gift of money pressed upon him by Futsing Christians.
He stipulated that it was to be used to create an educational scholarship fund in the memory of Lieutenant
Morris Cope Caldwell, third son of a China Coast family.
The fund begun that day, and added to since, is now
deposited in a bank in Tennessee, held against the day
when young Chinese may again come from the China
Coast to study in America.

Fukien seemed empty and lonely after the evacuation,
but there was work to do. The Japanese landed near
Futsing in September and occupied the city. They were
driving down from the North, and on the move all
through China. I called on the magistrate to ascertain his
plans and was assured that a mountain hideout had been
prepared, and that I would have a place there if the city
fell.

But the stream that ran under my Nanping office and
living quarters was my undoing. Recurring attacks of
malaria proved too much. It became obvious that I could
not safely stay on much longer. I was ordered to proceed
westward towards America.

I traveled one hundred miles up the north branch of

the Min to Kienyang where the U. S. Navy had a station of guerilla fighters. The Navy had a number of sick personnel whom it was taking out by truck. I hitched a ride with them to the airfield at Kangchow, three days and almost four hundred miles away. In Kangchow I boarded a 14th Air Force transport plane and headed for Kweilin. We spent the night there amidst air raids and the glow of the burning city a few miles away. The base was lost to the enemy the evening of the day I left for Kunming, Karachi, and America.

When one evacuates in the face of an advancing enemy, few gifts can be taken along. I did save a few little things, scrolls, inscribed pictures, and a porcelain figure, the gift of a Chinese general. Inscribed on it in the general's own brush strokes was a little legend applying, I thought, to the whole Caldwell family:

> *"Our sacred friendship glows freely from one to the other. Together we are fighting the wicked power of aggression in the world. Toiling for reconstruction of an ever-lasting peace and forging ahead...."*

14

THE CURTAIN
FALLS

THERE was an illusion of peace; the Japanese surrendered and victory came, and there was great rejoicing. Millions of Chinese began to move from the interior back to their homes on the China Coast. Families separated for four and five years were reunited. Refugee universities began the long trek home. Missionary families returned to the old stations.

Muriel and John were among those who finally came home when the Anglo-Chinese College in which they were teaching moved down the Min River to take up again its abode on the old campus in Foochow. Fukien Christian University and Hwa-Nan College returned. Father and Mother, too, for a time planned to return to

Futsing. But the threatening advance of the Chinese Communists made it impossible for them.

Shortly after the end of the war it was my privilege to spend six weeks in China, my task to travel through the country establishing the post-war Voice of America program. Later that year I returned again, to become Director of the United States Information Service, and to be a member of the American Embassy and the Marshall Mission. My official duties took me throughout China and even to Formosa. It was not difficult for me to find reasons to visit Foochow and Futsing, take one last hunting trip with Da Da, and stay again in Deng-Po's village high in the mountains west of my birth place.

The long years of war had changed many things, had almost changed the way of living. China's merchant fleet was gone. Only a few ancient river tubs remained to serve the China Coast ports. The highways along the coast, destroyed during the early days of the war, had not been rebuilt. But in the place of the old ways of traveling there was something new. The dreams of Timothy Richards, Baptist missionary of another century, had come true. Foochow, Amoy, Swatow, all the ports along the coast were served by airlines. A rough airfield had been hewn from the olive groves and rice paddies south of the foreign settlement in Foochow. One could fly into Foochow from Shanghai in less than three hours' time, could then travel on to Formosa or south to the other China Coast cities. The new airlines extended throughout the land, even into the far north and the frontier country to the west.

There were other changes along the coast. The houses in the Methodist Compound, near the cemeteries of Foochow, were now but shells. Foochow, as most other Chinese cities, had changed hands time and again during the war. As the Japanese were driven out, or left of their own accord, there were periods of anarchism and lawlessness. Houses were looted and burned, property carted away before order could be restored. On all of Nantai Island there was hardly a handful of habitable American and British houses.

In spite of these losses, in spite of mounting inflation, the missionary enterprise began slowly to move forward again. Missionaries were soon living in Futsing, in Nanping, in Hingwha. Schools and colleges were opened; churches were full to overflowing.

The year 1947 was a big year for the Land of Happiness. For it marked the end of the first century, the beginning of the second century of Methodist work. A vast centennial celebration took place in Foochow. Important people came from America, from all over China, from other Far Eastern nations. Four Methodist bishops were present, including Bishop Carleton Lacy. Sister denominations sent high ranking representatives to take part, to offer congratulations.

Chiang Kai Shek, Methodism's most illustrious convert, busy with a new war, took time to send a message. It said in part:

"During this period of atheistic, materialistic aggression, numerous bad influences have unfortunately entered our society. But we are determined that no difficulties of the past ten years, nor those confronting us now, shall be allowed to discourage the Christian Church nor retard its progress."

But Chiang Kai Shek was overly optimistic in his hope to withstand Communism. Preoccupied by the work of winning a great war, we had listened to false prophets who persuaded us that the ills of China, resulting in large part from the dislocations of an eight-year struggle, were ills that could be cured only by the new ideology. While we had fought, and died, and slept, a new enemy had grown greatly in strength.

Through 1947 and 1948, the Communists pushed ever more deeply into China. They crossed the Yangtse, spilling into the south and southwest. A few missionaries, courageous souls and not knowing what lay ahead, stayed on.

By the middle of 1949, all of China was imperiled. All over the land Americans and Chinese alike were faced with the decision to stay on or to flee, among them John and Muriel. A Communist friend assured them that they could stay on in peace, that "these people will treat you right." But with three children to think of, they wisely decided to join the refugees, once again to be evacuated. In May of 1949, they sailed southward for Hong Kong. They were the last of our clan on the China Coast.

Other missionaries all over China stayed, believing those who said the new rulers were reformers, interested only in the good of the people.

But always the pattern was the same: politeness and a degree of cooperation at first, slow but steadily growing pressure, gradual confiscation of property and human freedoms, increasing arrests of church leaders, brain washing, and execution. The missionaries who wished to leave were often allowed to do so, after months of waiting for exit permits, months often spent under house arrest or in jail.

Bishop Carleton Lacy was among those who applied for an exit permit, but were refused. The bishop's crime was well known about Foochow. At Conference time he had failed to reappoint a Chinese minister who had been guilty of dereliction in his church duties. For this Carleton Lacy was placed under arrest, charged with denying a livelihood to a citizen of the Peoples' Republic. There were other arrests, based upon similar flimsy charges, all with the intent of embarrassing and degrading Americans in the sight of the people with whom they had lived and worked for so long. The new rulers of the land could not afford to have men about who, like the bandit of Father's time, might say, "He is an American and a missionary. We can trust him."

The experience of those who stayed on and lived to see the free world again is well known now. Father Mark Tennien, a Maryknoll priest, and Olin Stockwell, Methodist missionary, are but two of the many who have written of their life in prison, of the brain-washing and persecution they suffered. In all of China today there is but a tiny handful of missionaries left. On all the China Coast, as far as I know, there is now not one American. The curtain has dropped, the light gone out all over China.

One wonders if the years of sacrifice were worth it, if there is any hope ahead. Can any bit of interest in Christianity, any residue of the once great prestige of America remain; if any remains, can it be sustained? Or is all lost?

The answer may lie in those little stories that come out of China today, and in how America reacts to these stories.

A missionary in Shanghai, denounced for weeks and months, in daily fear of house arrest, had feared to leave his home for a long period. When at last he and his wife went out again, to buy food in the markets, to walk the streets again, they were afraid of what reception they would receive. They need not have feared. For although there were no words of encouragement, sometimes not even a nod of recognition, there was in many places a simple gesture, a gesture needing no accompanying words: Chinese merchants, rickshaw coolies, church members with a simple thumbs up gesture bade the missionaries be at peace.

A lonely missionary wife lay ill in a China Coast hospital. Chinese friends were afraid to call upon her. But each day a simple cleaning man was allowed to come into her room. He moved about the floor, mopping and cleaning. And each day as he approached the bed he would begin to mumble in a pidgeon-English monotone, "Mao-Tse Tung, he no good; Mao-Tse Tung, he no good."

At Futsing where there was once a vigorous Christian community, where outstanding young Chinese entered the Christian ministry, many churches are closed. Most of the ministers have been driven underground, imprisoned, or executed. But the churches that are still open are functioning much as before, with women pastors. There are women district superintendents now. On a quiet Sunday night one can stand on a hill top in Futsing, in Foochow, in Nanping, in any one of a score of mission stations, and hear snatches of hymns from homes throughout the city. Like the Christian martyrs of two thousand years ago, many Chinese are worshiping in their homes, in little groups, perhaps without trained ministers, but with a simple dedication that has not yet been destroyed.

It is only among the young that the influence of a century of American friendship has perished. The children of China, taught to spy and to hate, their minds continually washed and poisoned, may be lost. In the face of five years' teaching about imperialistic, brutal, money-mad, war-mongering Americans they may have little memory of anything different.

But as long as there still are thousands who do remember, as long as there are men like Da Da, like the river boatman who took Father down the turbulent Min River because he was an American who needed help, as long as there are bandit chiefs who once said, "He is an American. We can trust him"—as long as there are men and women who saw America at its best, there is hope.

And in the work of the American China Coast families, China did see America at its best, saw perhaps the real inner strength that has made America great. Is it too much to think that perhaps in the work of the Lacys, the Worleys, the Burkes, the Caldwells there may even be a lesson for America?

America has spent billions overseas since the end of the War. We have had mutual assistance, economic assistance, military assistance, and technical assistance programs. As I am writing this story of the China Coast, there are 185,000 Americans, employed by seventy bureaus and departments of our government, all engaged in some manner of assistance abroad. That is many, many times the highest total of Protestant and Catholic missionaries ever engaged in foreign work at one time. Yet in spite of this vast army of men and women, whose job is after all to sell democracy and fight Communism, the forces of the West seem always to be on the defensive, always to be pushing back, not forward.

I believe two great lessons might be learned from the missionaries, lessons which might somehow stem the tide, and develop again an offensive of the American spirit.

First, the missionaries had something that has been sadly lacking among the ranks of those who labor for the American Government on the world's frontiers today. They had what I would call the missing ingredient. When Father and Mother left Tennessee for China at the turn of the century, it must have been like a trip to the moon—especially for Mother. For the China of 1900 was a land of hatred and suspicion, of disease and misrule. Living accommodations were bad, travel uncomfortable

and dangerous, customs outlandish and cruel. Yet
Mother, and the hundreds of missionary women who
came before her and have labored since, were able to live
and work and be happy.

The missionaries had no mansions in which to live, no
PX's and vast commissaries in which to buy their sup-
plies, no beautiful restaurants or cafés in which to take
refreshments, no cars to travel, indeed no roads on which
cars could operate. In spite of these difficulties these men
and women of all faiths and denominations did succeed in
making friends where America's official billions have
often failed. They succeeded in breaking down the walls
of hatred and superstition, in banishing age-old customs,
in building the very foundations of democracy which we
seek now to bolster and defend. They succeeded because
they lived close to the people, because they learned the
languages and the customs, because they lived not only in
the great cities but in fishing villages and mountain ham-
lets throughout Asia. But above all they succeeded because they had that missing ingredient—*a spirit of dedication*. It was so strong and shining that it broke down
the walls of hatred and superstition, so unmistakable that
the cries of imperialism and exploitation fell on deaf ears.
Without that spirit of dedication there can be no victory
over Communism, no real peace.

And then, those people all over the world who are most
susceptible to Communism are the men and women who
have always lived in poverty and fear. The poverty and
the fear are often a part of their religions and their cul-

ture. Men who worship a hundred devils, who must placate those devils, whose day to day existence is shaped by fear, cannot have the same outlook we Americans have. Fear begets hatred and suspicion, poverty, and disease. Is it enough simply to show a farmer in China or Korea or India new methods of agriculture? Must not fear and evil, devil worship, and ancient customs be changed before the farmer can make his new knowledge work for him and for his people, before he can understand the true meaning of democracy, before he can himself begin to build a democratic society?